Magrey R. deVega

D0735390

EMBRACING THE UNCERTAIN

40 Devotions for Unsteady Times

Abingdon Press / Nashville

Embracing the Uncertain
40 Devotions for Unsteady Times

Copyright © 2017 Abingdon Press
All rights reserved.

This book is printed on elemental chlorine-free paper.
Library of Congress Cataloging-in-Publication Data has been requested.
ISBN 978-1-5018-48094

17 18 19 20 21 22 23 24 25 26 — 10 9 8 7 6 5 4 3 2 1
MANUFACTURED IN THE UNITED STATES OF AMERICA

TABLE OF CONTENTS

INTRODUCTION

I am a creature of routine, particularly in the mornings. I do my best to wake up at the same time each day, fix breakfast for my two daughters, pack their lunches, and get myself ready. We are generally out the door and in the car at the same time every morning, driving the same route every day to school, to the point where I can visualize every landmark and every turn in my mind. Familiarity breeds predictability, which in turn produces reliability.

And reliability brings comfort.

The season of Lent is for many of us a lot like a well-worn morning routine. Many of us have heard these stories so many times that we know the destination before we even begin the journey. It's true that Ash Wednesday and Lent move around from year to year, but the essential path through Lent is the same. As we begin to retrace the post-Transfiguration stories in the Gospels, we know we are heading toward Jerusalem. We anticipate the throngs of Hosanna-shouting masses on Palm Sunday. We have been to the upper room to witness the drama of Maundy Thursday. We are veterans of many Good Fridays past, and we know what to expect on Easter morning.

The challenge, then, is to try to discover something new and compelling about the stories of Lent this time around, particularly when our lives feel so uncertain. These passages may be familiar, and the rhythm of the season so reliable, but we know that our futures are anything but. These stories are timeless, but as our situations change from year to year, we find ourselves living on tectonic plates of shifting change within us and around us.

Embracing the Uncertain: 40 Devotions for Unsteady Times invites you to take a fresh look at these familiar stories and to discover new truths amid the uncertainty of your life. The daily devotions follow a timeline of events, beginning with the descent of Jesus and the disciples from the Transfiguration and ending with the passion of Holy Week and the glory of Easter.

On some days, you will be asked to read the same story as recorded by more than one Gospel writer, so that you can see the similarities and differences in their perspectives. Each entry will conclude with a question for your own personal reflection or perhaps group discussion. You may find that your Lenten journey will be greatly enhanced if you undertake it with other trusted companions along the way.

This devotional can also integrate with the weekly study, *Embracing the Uncertain: A Lenten Study for Unsteady Times*, which goes further in depth into stories not covered by this devotional. Between these two books, you will be able to read and study all the major post-Transfiguration stories from all four Gospels.

Ultimately, I hope that this Lenten season will be much more than a retracing of familiar territory. May you find new insights in these stories that will illuminate the current situations you face, and may God draw you further along a path of commitment that will lead to your full obedience and surrender to Jesus Christ.

It is my prayer that this Lenten season will be a blessed one for you, even amid your uncertainties.

Welcome to the journey.

DAY 1

Mark 9:2-13

YOU SHOULDN'T STAY AND SHOULDN'T GO NOW

The transfiguration of Jesus is the pivot point in the Gospel story. From here on, Jesus is no longer simply the miracle healer or the prolific teacher. He turns his face to the cross and marches into his mission to be the Messiah, who gives himself up to be arrested, tortured, and put to death.

These matters are all lost on the disciples, of course; you can tell by their reaction when Jesus is transformed on the mountain.

"Jesus, this is great!" Peter said, in a manner of speaking. "This is awesome! I have an idea, let's stay here on this mountain forever! We'll set up three tents, one each for you, Elijah, and Moses. Imagine it! A veritable amusement park of faithful heroes! People will stream in from everywhere to catch a glimpse, get an autograph, and take a selfie. Move over, Comic Con, this will be the place where everyone will want to be. Let's stay here!"

But that was not Jesus' desire. He knew they weren't going to stay forever.

The disciples might have assumed then that Jesus was thinking in the opposite direction. "Well, great, then let's go share this story with the whole world," they may have thought. "The people in Capernaum aren't going to believe this! The *Nazareth Chronicle Times* will eat this story up, and the *Bethlehem Bugle* is going to love it too. We'll book an agent, go on a speaking tour, and maybe—if we're lucky—we'll get to go on *Oprah!* The whole world must know about this. Let's go!"

But Jesus said no; he told them not to tell anybody until after he had risen from the dead (Mark 9:9).

So, let's get this straight, Jesus. We can't stay on the mountain and keep the story to ourselves. We can't leave the mountain and tell other people. What do you want us to do? We can't stay, we can't leave. What, then?!

That is the question we ask on the cusp of Lent. The answer we find in this story is the reason the Transfiguration account is so important. Jesus' transformation not only reminds us of our past and refocuses us on our future; it also invites us to incorporate this one critical ingredient into our daily spiritual lives: the practice of watching.

Jesus wanted his disciples to watch.

You're not yet ready to share this story, Jesus would tell them, because you have not yet seen all there is to see. Not until you see the cross, and not until you see God's divine love revealed through death and resurrection, will you be able to understand all the mysteries of the faith.

The reminder here for you and me as we enter these special, sacred forty days is to watch—to carefully attune our attention to the Spirit of God at work in our lives.

For most of us, that is precisely the missing ingredient, the one thing that is preventing our good life from being a deep life. It's what prevents a successful life, a prosperous life, and a life of achievement from being a life of real purpose and eternal significance.

What many of us are missing is the disciplined practice of constant attention to spiritual things, watching and listening and praying for God's best aims for us and for the world.

You see, a lot of times we are like the disciples. We may say, "Lord, it is good for us to be here" and wish to stay in the past. We dwell on the glory days and never really let go of the things that have already happened. Or we may want to rush into the future, saying, "I've got it, God. I know what I'm supposed to do with my life: my job, my family, my school, my career, my future. I know." We rush on ahead, charging forward, eager and energized.

Neither of these is the way that leads to deep significance and eternal impact. Instead, we have to *watch*. That means praying. And a lot of asking. And a lot of listening. We must pray, asking God to reveal to us how we are to live and behave and talk and relate to each other, and we must be willing to listen patiently for God's response.

And yes, it means going to a cross. It means going to a place where our old patterns of behavior and our old perspectives and prejudices— our old selves—can be put to death.

Over these next forty days, we will follow Jesus down from the mountain and walk the paths where he leads us. As we trace the post-Transfiguration stories of the Gospels, we'll pay attention to the cadence of his steps and watch his footprints, so that we don't scurry ahead of him or lag behind.

Along the way, listen up. Pay attention. Watch. Discover the work of the Holy Spirit within you, pointing out parts of your life that you would much rather ignore. Receive encouragement and affirmation from the most unsuspecting sources, which is one of God's favorite ways to relate to us.

The entire time, ask God the same question the disciples asked of Jesus in the wake of his Transfiguration: What does it mean to rise from the dead?

God, help me to walk in your path and follow your lead. Teach me not to rush ahead of you and not to lag behind. Teach me to watch. Amen.

In what ways are you fixated on your past, either reliving past hurts or clinging to past achievements?

DAY 2

Matthew 17:14-21; Mark 9:14-29; Luke 9:37-43

PRAYER IS SIMPLE BUT NOT EASY

I will admit that there are many statements Jesus made that I have yet to understand completely. One of them is in Mark 9:29. The presenting story is of the father who came to Jesus and the disciples so that his demon-possessed son could be healed. The deeper story is in why the disciples were not able to heal him.

After Jesus healed the boy, the disciples were left wondering why they could not cast the demon out themselves (Mark 9:28). They were doing everything right, or so they thought. They said the right words, performed the right motions, and followed the formulas to the letter. But apparently, they couldn't do what Jesus could do.

The answer Jesus gives is that they weren't praying: "Throwing this kind of spirit out requires prayer" (Mark 9:29).

That is a good response, to a certain degree. Prayer, we have learned, involves our surrender to God, an invocation of the power of the Holy Spirit, and a declaration of belief that God can do what we cannot do. Because we are followers of Jesus, every action, thought, and aspect of our being ought to be centered and grounded in a spirit of prayer. It should not surprise us that Jesus answers the question in this way.

But it doesn't make his answer any easier to understand. It seems like he's saying prayer alone would guarantee success in spiritual endeavors. If the disciples had only prayed, they could have cast the demon out.

Back in 2000, acclaimed sports columnist Rick Reilly reflected on two separate accidents involving famous NFL football players Isaac Bruce and Derrick Thomas. Bruce's car flipped over, but he was able to walk away unscathed. Thomas's car accident, however, resulted in

Thomas being paralyzed, and he ultimately passed away a few weeks later.

In the February 7, 2000, issue of *Sports Illustrated*, Reilly interviewed Isaac Bruce, before Derrick Thomas died:

> "Do you ever think about Thomas and say, 'That could be me'?" I ask Bruce.
>
> "Oh, no, not at all," Bruce says.
>
> "Why not?" I ask.
>
> "Because as I was flipping, I threw my hands off the wheel and called Jesus' name."
>
> "Does that mean God doesn't love Derrick Thomas?" I ask.
>
> "Oh, no," Bruce says. "I don't know what Derrick said as his car was flipping."[1]

In the interview, Reilly continued to press Isaac Bruce about other individuals who were Christian and had nevertheless perished in tragic ways. Bruce appeared unwilling to accept the possibility that people don't always get what they pray for. I don't want to fault him too much, especially if he were to interpret Mark 9:29 the way many people have. He believes in the power of prayer; there is no blame in that. But we can see the danger in simplifying Christian belief and practice to the point where it is rendered useless—and even harmful—in the face of real life complexities.

In fact, I don't think Jesus would say that prayer is simple at all. What if his response to the disciples was not simply, "If you had just prayed, it would have worked" but, "If you only knew what you were up against, you would not have tried to do it on your own to begin with." In other words, Jesus' call to prayer would have been a reminder that complicated times require a God beyond our comprehension. The forces of suffering and evil are so overwhelming that we dare not think we can handle them on our own.

Maybe that's what prayer really is, after all. It's not some magical incantation that gives us what we want when we want it. It's a reminder that when life comes at us hard, we can't go at it alone.

God, teach me to trust in you, that I might not face my struggles alone. Teach me how to pray. Amen.

When have you ever struggled with your prayer life? What do you think happens when you pray?

---

1 Rick Reilly, "Two Men, Two Flips of Fate," *Sports Illustrated*, February 7, 2000, https://www.si.com/vault/2000/02/07/273385/two-men-two-flips-of-fate. Accessed October 6, 2017.

DAY 3

Matthew 17:22-23; Mark 9:30-32; Luke 9:43-45

THE BEST WORST ADVICE EVER

If you read all three versions of this short conversation between Jesus and his disciples, you will discover some subtle but significant differences among Matthew, Mark, and Luke. All three agree on the gist of the conversation: while in Galilee, Jesus predicts his death, telling the disciples that he would be handed over to the authorities.

The difference lies in the way the three Gospel writers portray the reaction of the disciples and their state of mind.

In Matthew, the disciples' reaction is the simplest and most straightforward. "And they were heartbroken" (Matthew 17:23). That's it. The disciples were heartbroken by Jesus' words. No elaboration, no explanation.

Now skip over to Mark. Mark was written before either Matthew or Luke, and it often offers the shorter version of a particular Gospel story, which the other two writers embellish and expand. In this instance, though, Mark actually gives us a slightly fuller picture than Matthew of what the disciples were wondering: "They didn't understand this kind of talk, and they were afraid to ask him" (Mark 9:32). They were not only confused about what Jesus was saying, but they were also afraid even to ask him about it.

Now look at Luke. It's here that we get the most complex and most mystifying psychological profile of the disciples at that moment. First, Jesus prefaces his comment with the words, "Take these words to heart…" (Luke 9:44). In other words, listen up, disciples. Pay attention. Let these words sink in deep. Jesus goes out of his way to perk up their ears and tell them that his next words are very important.

At the same time, Luke tells us not only that the disciples did not understand Jesus' statement and that they were afraid to ask him about it, but Luke also tells us that "its meaning was hidden from them" (Luke 9:45).

Whew, that just brings up a whole lot of questions, doesn't it? Who or what did the hiding? Was it God? Was it the world? Was it their own finite comprehension? Did Jesus know they would not be able to understand what he was saying to them about his arrest and crucifixion? If he did, then why bother telling them at all? Why did he even tell them to "take this to heart" if they weren't going to understand it to begin with?

Oh, it had to be hard to be a disciple sometimes. It would have been hard enough to understand what Jesus was saying, but then to have the meaning concealed from them? Yikes. It must have felt like the chips had just been stacked against them.

When I was much younger, I was having a conversation with my dad. I don't remember the exact circumstances, but I'd had a very rough day at school. Things were not going well with something or another, and I came home just weepy.

My dad sat me down at the dining room table and listened to how my day went. He was often a man of few words, especially in moments like these, but it was helpful just to empty out my emotions in front of him.

When I was finished, we sort of sat in silence for a few seconds. I'm not sure what I was expecting him to say, but I was hoping he would say something encouraging, something like, "It's okay, son. You'll be fine." Or, "I know you're strong, you'll make it through this." Or, "Don't worry, this will pass."

Instead, he looked at me in much the same way Jesus must have looked at his disciples to get them to take his word to heart. Then he said this: "You know what, son? You're going to have a lot tougher problems than this as you grow older."

I chuckle even now as I type this. I remember thinking, "That's the craziest, most unsuitable advice I have ever heard, Dad. Thanks a lot." The last thing I wanted to hear, as I felt like I was careening downhill, is that there were steeper slopes and rocks ahead. If that's what the disciples experienced when Jesus told them he would be arrested and killed, it's no wonder they were confused, distressed, and afraid to ask Jesus more.

But *now*, I can see exactly the great wisdom my father was sharing with me. He was right. There have been so many other hurdles and trials in my life that I can't even remember what I was so worried about when he and I had that talk. Oddly enough, his words at the time were strangely comforting. In retrospect, it was exactly what I needed to hear.

My youth, inexperience, and inability to see the high-altitude view of life concealed the meaning of my dad's profound wisdom. It would only be revealed to me when the true sufferings of life hit me. If Luke were my autobiographer, he would say that it was not until I followed Jesus to the cross that I could discover the beauty of God's resurrection.

It is that same resurrecting power of God that enabled me to go through some very difficult times and revealed to me the wisdom of my father's words. Such can be the case for you too.

God, thank you for being with me, even during the toughest times, even when I feel confused and heartbroken. Help me to trust you, especially when I don't understand fully what I am going through. Amen.

What is the best advice you ever received from someone, only to understand and appreciate it more fully in retrospect?

DAY 4

Matthew 17:24-27

TEMPLE TAXES AND FISHY COINS

Matthew, Mark, and Luke all agree that after yesterday's story about Jesus predicting his death, there was tomorrow's story about the disciples arguing about who among them was the greatest. But Matthew alone tucks between them this odd—very odd—story about Jesus telling Peter to go fishing for a coin-bearing fish.

On the surface, this is a dispute about paying taxes. It's not the official Roman tax, the kind that got Jesus into a heated discussion elsewhere in the Gospels about whose head was on the Roman coin (Matthew 22:15-22; Mark 12:13-17; Luke 20:20-26). This is not about whether to pay taxes to the IRS. Instead, this about whether Jesus ought to pay the *temple* tax—his contribution to the treasury of the temple in order to support its ongoing work.

Certainly, we would believe that Peter answered the question correctly. Yes, his teacher paid the temple tax. That should have been it. End of story. On to the next Scripture passage.

But the story stretches on, with Jesus speaking to Peter as they came into the house where Jesus and Peter were staying. The two of them had a cryptic conversation about kings, the king's children, taxes, and fish with coins in their mouths. What Jesus said to Peter, in essence, was that the kings of the world don't expect their *children* to pay taxes. Only the strangers.

Whoa. What exactly was Jesus saying here? Was he telling Peter he shouldn't have to pay the half-shekel temple tax? And if he did, what does that say to us? Should we not be supporting our churches? What about financial stewardship, and tithing, and giving a portion of our income, and offering ourselves in gratitude to God, and funding the missions and ministries of the...

…OK, let's not get out of hand.

It might be helpful to remember the community to which Matthew was originally writing his Gospel. Most scholars agree that Matthew was writing to a community in or near the ancient city of Antioch, in modern day Turkey. Archaeologists have discovered ruins indicating that in Antioch, villages contained homes of Jewish people sitting right next to homes of early Christians who were once Jews. In other words, it would not have been unusual for Jews to have Jewish-Christians as their neighbors. This story in Matthew would indicate to us that there must have been some fascinating conversations among neighbors in that city.

"So, neighbor, did you head up to Jerusalem and pay your temple tax?"

"Me? No, I don't have to. See, I follow Jesus now."

"Yeah, but you're Jewish, aren't you?"

"Well, it's complicated. See, everything I believe about Jesus is based on Judaism, but I'm not exactly Jewish. I don't know. I'm trying to figure it out."

"Well, are you circumcised?"

"Yes, but I'm not sure about the kosher thing."

"What? Listen, you're going to have to figure this thing out. I'm not sure what to make of you."

"I know. But look, I don't want to cause problems between us. We worship the same God, right? We're friends, right?"

"Yeah. But it's complicated."

Well, if that's the kind of thing that was happening in Matthew's day, then this teaching from Jesus is not as much about whether to give to the church, just like it's not about going fishing and expecting to win the lottery. What this is about is interreligious dialogue, between two groups of people who were trying to figure out their relationship with each other, and, in the case of the early Jewish-Christians, trying to figure out their own relationship to their Hebrew roots.

Seen in this way, this text can offer us a hopeful word, not a divisive one. Jesus asked Peter, "From whom do earthly kings collect taxes, from their children or from strangers?" (Matthew 17:25). If we see for a moment that the financial support of the temple was a privilege, and not a punishment, then the fact that the right answer was "the stranger" means that Jesus was stretching the reach of God's grace to those on the outside.

Remember, this is the same Gospel that alone includes the parable of the laborers of the vineyard, in which those who worked the shortest hours were paid the same as those who labored from the beginning (Matthew 20:1-16). In the economics of the kingdom, grace is not based on merit or seniority, but only on the goodness of God. God favors all people, regardless of who they are or who they have been, and seeks to widen the boundaries of the Kingdom to include as many people as possible.

Just how abundant is that grace? It's so abundant that you could receive it in the most unexpected places, in the most undeserving ways.

Like in the mouth of a fish.

God, thank you for your grace, which is given to me without regard to merit or fault. Help me to be part of the expansion of your Kingdom, to reach out in love to all people, everywhere. Amen.

Have you ever developed friendships with people whose faith is different from yours? Not just different denominations or Christian traditions, but people of other religions? If not, what has prevented you from doing so? If so, what have been the benefits and challenges?

DAY 5

Matthew 18:1-5; Mark 9:33-37; Luke 9:46-50

WHO IS THE GREATEST?

Have you ever been in a classroom where the teacher called out a disruption? The instructor was lecturing in front of the class—maybe speaking from a podium, or writing on a chalkboard, sharing some grand truth or little nugget of wisdom—only to stop, notice some chatter in the background and say to those kids, "Would you like to share with the rest of the class what it is you're discussing?" The students were stunned silent. They were caught red-handed. They have been found out, and now they must make amends. I won't ask for a poll, but I wonder how many of you know this scenario firsthand.

Much like those students, Jesus' disciples were caught. Jesus was sharing with them the most amazing news they would ever hear, about how they would have a front-row seat to the greatest moment in human history. They were going to see the salvation of God before their very eyes.

But they missed it. They were too busy being embroiled in their own squabbles.

They were arguing about who the greatest among them was. They were competing for Jesus' attention, debating who should get to sit on Jesus' right hand when the new Kingdom came. They were fussing over who would get to be second-in-command and trying to one-up each other for greatness in the Kingdom.

Here's an important nugget of truth: any time we get swept up into petty divisions over who is great and who is more worthy of attention, we miss it. When we get caught debating whose opinions count more and whose gripes aren't given attention, we miss it.

We miss a chance to see Jesus in glory. We miss an opportunity for God to share with us something bold and exciting, a vision of the future, hope for tomorrow. Every time we get caught up in ourselves, we miss a chance to hear God's voice.

What Jesus said to the disciples, he also says to us today: "Whoever wants to be first must be least of all and the servant of all" (Mark 9:35).

If you want to be truly great in the Kingdom, it's not about how many people are below you. It is about how many people are above you.

If you truly want the attention of our heavenly parent, it's not about how many people serve you but about how many people you serve.

If you want to be first, you must be last. It's not about the glory you get. It's about the glory God gets through you.

In his book *Written in Blood*, Robert Coleman includes the moving story of a little boy and his sister. The boy had had a dreaded disease and had been wonderfully delivered from death. He had been immunized against the disease. But the same immunization did not work on his sister and she was dying.

The physician, realizing she needed a transfusion of the boy's blood (a fair amount of it), called the boy aside and asked him if he would be willing.

"Would you give your blood?" the doctor asked. The little boy's lips trembled and he hesitated for a moment, looked out the window, and thought. Then he replied, "Yes, I'll do it." They took the brother and the sister into a room, and the blood began to be transferred. It was like a miracle. Life came back to her body.

After a while, the doctor came in and the little boy looked up and asked the doctor, "When do I die?" The doctor understood why the boy's lips had trembled and why there was a moment of hesitation. He thought he would die, when all the doctor wanted was a little bit of his blood. But he was willing to give his life so that his sister might live.[1]

This is how brothers and sisters in the Kingdom should live together—not in competition but through servanthood, being the least and servant of all, not seeking first place.

The challenge is clear. How can you assume the mentality of a servant? How will you work to praise and honor others instead of yourself? How will we function together so that God is glorified instead of you?

God, forgive me for the times I have put myself before you and others, and fought with others out of competition and jealousy. Teach me to have the mind of Christ, that I might be a servant of others. Amen.

When are you most prone to squabbling with other Christians and missing something glorious that God is doing?

---

1 Robert Emerson Coleman, *Written in Blood: A Devotional Bible Study of the Blood of Christ* (Old Tappan, NJ: Revell, 1972), na.

DAY 6

Matthew 18:6-9; Mark 9:38-48; Luke 9:49-50

DRAW THE CIRCLE WIDER

Oh, those poor disciples.

Just a few verses prior in Matthew, Mark, and Luke, we read a story of how the disciples were unable to heal a demon-possessed boy, and we could sense their confusion and embarrassment. But this story just rubs salt in their wounds and smacks their already bruised egos. They witnessed a stranger able to do what they knew they could not: cast out a demon.

They went to Jesus to tell him, but we do not know why. Maybe they were wanting to complain: Jesus, did you know about this guy? He acts like you, claims to do so in your name, but for all we know, he is an impostor. Or maybe they were wanting to complain more to Jesus, admitting their own inadequacies: Jesus, what's going on here? We are the ones struggling with doing these miracles, and now this ringer comes in and acts like it's a piece of cake! What's going on here?

We don't know disciples' exact motivation, but we are certain about their tone. You can tell by what they said: "Teacher, we saw someone throwing demons out in your name, and we tried to stop him because he wasn't following us" (Mark 9:38).

We tried to stop him, because he wasn't following . . . *us.*

That is the point where we might imagine Jesus saying, "Okay, wait a minute. What is this *us* business?"

The disciples were fixated on the fact that this person, whoever he was, was not an official part of the gang. He didn't wear their team jersey. He wasn't a card-carrying member of their union. He couldn't produce the official paperwork. Therefore, the disciples not only thought he wasn't one of them, they thought he wasn't worthy to *be* one of them.

In David Toycen's book *The Power of Generosity: How to Transform Yourself and Your World*, Toycen tells the story of Stan Mooneyham. Mooneyham is a former director of World Vision, a charitable agency that combats global poverty and hunger. At a national gathering of religious leaders from a wide spectrum of faith traditions—Catholic and Protestant, conservative and liberal—Mooneyham was facilitating discussions when conversations quickly devolved into fractious arguments. At the end of the first day of meetings, a weary Mooneyham was ready to relinquish to someone else the role of leadership in these circumstances.

Instead, the next day, an inspired Mooneyham turned to a flip chart and drew a number of little dots, each with a circle around them. He told the bickering leaders that this was how they perceived themselves and their relationships with others—as isolated individuals hedged by self-protection.

Then, Mooneyham drew a large, all-encompassing circle around all the dots, and read a portion of Edwin Markhams's poem, "Outwitted." The poem begins with the drawing of a circle that defines who was in and who was out. But then he says,

> But Love and I had the wit to win:
> We drew a circle that took him in.

Mooneyham concluded, "I may not be in your circle, but you are in mine, and there is nothing you can do to get out. You can't resign, walk out, or run away. If you try it, I will just draw a bigger circle."[1]

Immediately, the bitterness and strain in the room evaporated as people recognized their own protective bubbles and remembered that God's wide circle included everyone in the whole world. Starting that day and for the rest of their time together, Mooneyham and the religious leaders had the most productive time building relationships that World Vision had ever encountered.

I wonder sometimes if God looks at the global church and wearies of its divisions. Disagreements over doctrine, polity, and liturgy seem to spawn more division and less dialogue, more cracks and less common understanding. We all tend to draw circles defining who's in and who's out. Inevitably, we draw those circles around ourselves.

Again, we imagine Jesus telling his disciples, "What is this *us* business? Since when has it ever been about people following *us*? This is about following *me*." This us vs. them mentality may be common in the world, but it has no place in the Kingdom.

It is in these moments that we can remember the words of the hymn "There's a Wideness in God's Mercy":

> For the love of God is broader
> than the measure of our mind;
> and the heart of the Eternal
> is most wonderfully kind.
>
> If our love were but more simple,
> we should rest upon God's word;
> and our lives would be illumined
> by the presence of our Lord.[2]

If God's mercy is so wide, and God's love so all-encompassing, why do we try so hard to monopolize it for ourselves? In the end, shouldn't our efforts to define who's right and who's wrong defer to the realization that we are all in this kingdom-building business together?

God, thank you for seeing me for who I am. Teach me to do the same in my relationships with others. Help me to be part of your work to bring all people together, in your love. Amen.

When was there a time in your life when your opinion of a person improved as you got to know the person better? How might God be calling you to tear down walls of prejudice in your relationships with other people?

1 David Toycen, *The Power of Generosity: How to Transform Yourself and Your World* (Waynesboro, GA: Authentic Media, 2004), 80-81.

2 "There's a Wideness in God's Mercy," Frederick W. Faber; *The United Methodist Hymnal* (Nashville: The United Methodist Publishing House 1989), 121, stanzas 3 and 4.

DAY 7

Luke 9:51-62; John 7:2-11

REALLY? RAIN DOWN FIRE?

Let's do a simple thought exercise.

What if Jesus had not died on the cross, but instead died of natural causes? Would he still be our Messiah? In other words, if Jesus had died of pneumonia, or the plague, or something other than the violence of the Crucifixion, would we still consider him our Lord and Savior? It might have meant he could have lived longer, into his elderly years, teaching and preaching and leaving behind a much more prolific public ministry than his mere three years. But would the manner of a natural death still have been salvific for us?

Judging from the way Luke describes it in the first sentence of this story, his answer would be an emphatic *no*. The importance of Jesus' death is communicated in Luke's Gospel not just in the way Jesus died, but in the motivation with which he met his death. Read again: "As the time approached when Jesus was to be taken up into heaven, he *determined to go* to Jerusalem" (Luke 9:51, emphasis added).

Luke wants to make it very clear to his readers that all that was about to happen to Jesus came from an act of his will. If there was to be a point when Jesus could turn away from his mission and choose another course, this would have been it. But instead, he determined to move forward voluntarily, and nothing was going to stand in the way of his fulfilling his mission. The fact that he did so willingly is itself a gift to us, for it gives us a model of self-sacrificial, self-giving love that can both inspire us and instruct us to do the same for others.

That reality, of course, was lost on the world at the time. That kind of self-sacrifice was as rare then as it is today, so it should not surprise us that the first reaction from the public was one of rejection.

Jesus sent out a group of messengers, a sort of advance team to promote and prepare the upcoming cities for Jesus' arrival (Luke 9:52). And the early reports from the region of Samaria were not favorable; because Jesus was headed for Jerusalem, the Samaritan towns refused to welcome him (9:53). The reason why should not be surprising.

Jews and Samaritans had a long, complicated cultural relationship, full of conflict and animosity. Both groups claimed the heritage of the Israelite people, and each group resented and rejected the claims of the other. These two groups both believed they were the true representation of the original Israelite monarchy and the keepers of Hebrew law. The Samaritans believed theirs alone was true and holy worship, and the Jews could see nothing in the Samaritans but a mixed-ethnicity dilution of pure Judaism.

For this reason, it should be no surprise to us that the Samaritans were less than friendly to the prospect of Jesus including their region among the tour stops on his way toward Jerusalem. It should also be no surprise that James and John were ready to strike back: "When the disciples James and John saw this, they said, 'Lord, do you want us to call fire down from heaven to consume them?'" (Luke 9:54).

Frankly, James and John's reaction would be utterly ridiculous if it weren't so human. "Hey, Jesus, since the Samaritans rejected us, would you like us to, uh, rain down some fire on them? Huh, Jesus? Whaddya say?"

Apparently, James and John somehow saw themselves as mafia thugs for hire, ready to do the godfather's bidding. Never mind the fact that there was no prior evidence that the disciples *could* rain down fire on people, or that Jesus ever *wanted* to rain down fire on people. But for some reason, these two disciples thought they could take a page out of a superhero comic book and exact revenge on their sworn cultural enemies.

Naturally, Jesus rebuked them. Jesus was not interested in stirring up animosity with the Samaritans, and there are many other stories in the Gospels to suggest that his mission was to save all people, regardless of ethnicity. Jesus' interaction with the woman at the well (John 4:1-30) and the parable of the good Samaritan (Luke 10:25-37) are the two most famous examples of how Jesus came to redeem people across all religious and cultural boundaries, including the Samaritans.

And about that fire from the sky...eventually, God would rain down fire. But in a very different way.

Luke, who is the only Gospel writer to record this knee-jerk response from James and John, is also the same writer who gave us the Book of Acts. There, on the Day of Pentecost, we do get fire from heaven. Fire came in the form of the Holy Spirit, who took all people, from all parts of the earth, and all different ethnicities, and formed one community (Acts 2:1-4).

Since its birth, the Church has been comprised of people from all walks of life. May we live into that same vision today.

God, thank you for the self-sacrificial, self-giving love of Jesus. Grant me the vision and the courage to reach out to others in the same way, even if they are different from me. Amen.

What difference does it make for you to remember that Jesus died willingly, for you?

DAY 8

Luke 10:1-24

TRAVELING LIGHTLY

Jesus offered the disciples a very simple prescription: travel lightly. As you go out into the mission field to do the work of the kingdom, do not carry excess baggage. Carry no wallet, no purse, no sandals.

It's odd advice, to be sure, except that it might just be the word you need to hear. Consider the possibility that you may be carrying too many burdens on your back at the moment. Burdens of shame about your past. Burdens of low self-esteem and feelings of inadequacy. Burdens of addiction, resentment, anger. Burdens of worry about a future you cannot control.

Try as we might, we cannot seem to let these burdens go.

I will admit to you that this is particularly hard for me. Amid the many backpacks and satchels I use to carry my various burdens around from moment to moment, the biggest one by far would be labeled "worry." It's emblazoned in a giant patch on the largest luggage, and I use it to lug around every little thing I am concerned about. I keep adding to it without even knowing. When I am at my unhealthiest, I can easily spin out worst-case scenarios that take me down a slippery slope of forecasting disaster long before it is even a possibility.

Here's an example. My two daughters and I were watching a show on television in which the two hosts were testing various theories on what to do if you accidentally drive your car into a body of water. With your car quickly sinking and submerging, what is the best thing to do to make sure you escape the car and survive?

Do you open the car door once you hit the water? No.

Do you try to roll down the window? No.

Do you wait until the car hits the bottom, then try to swim out of your car? No.

As it turns out, the best thing to do, according to the hosts of the show, is break the window using one of those car window hammers. Maybe you've heard of this hammer. It's a special tool that provides a lot of force in a precise point on the window, shattering the window and enabling you to swim out of the car quickly.

As soon as we saw that on the episode, I turned to the girls and said, "We need one of those in the car!" My daughters, Grace and Madelyn, said, "Yeah, we do!"

The next day, I went up the street to the local car parts store and bought a car window hammer, stuck it in the glove compartment, and felt totally prepared to beat the odds in the event of submerging the car in water.

Now, I should say…at the time, we were living in Iowa. We were thousands of miles from either ocean. The closest large lake was more than an hour away. The nearest body of water was an adorable little creek that for part of the year we could skip across.

But just in case, I was ready with my hammer!

There's nothing wrong with being prepared. Having plans in place in case disasters strike is not a bad thing at all. But there does come a point when the worry and anxiety about a future that may not come to pass becomes so burdensome that it prevents God's peace and joy in our lives.

In this Scripture passage, Jesus was trying to teach the disciples how to be free from worry, to trust in God. He was telling them to go out to do their work and simply trust that God would provide everything that they needed: what they would eat, where they would sleep, and how their other needs would be cared for. All of those extra burdens they were worried about were just slowing them down.

But that's not all. Jesus' message to the disciples was also to focus on the mission, which is to live the kind of self-giving, sacrificial life that honors God and serves others. When we are centered on doing the work that God has for us, then all of those burdens we think are important really don't matter in the long run.

What extra luggage do you have that you can lay down? What are those worries and concerns, that guilt and shame, that you have been lugging around far too long, for much too great a distance?

For the rest of this Lenten journey, shed some baggage. Jettison those burdens, those self-comforting habits, those rough edges of your personality, all of which pull your attention away from God. With those set aside, we can learn to rely upon God, to listen for the guidance of the Holy Spirit.

Travel lightly, strengthening your relationship with God and relying on God's Spirit to guide you.

God, thank you for giving me the strength and the wisdom to let go of my burdens. Teach me to trust in you. Amen.

What baggage are you carrying today? What do you think God is doing to strengthen and empower you to let go of that baggage?

DAY 9

Luke 10:25-37

DRAWING NEAR

If someone were to ask you the question, "What is the key to true life?" I suspect your answer would not include fame, or trophies, or riches. Deep down inside, we acknowledge that the things that matter most are relationships and that what matters most is love.

Fair enough.

But saying that love is the answer always prompts the follow-up question: What does it mean to love? When it comes to the nitty-gritty of life, how should we love others? Whom should we love? How much should we love them?

In other words, if the key to real life is love, what does real love look like?

Well, for Jesus, the answer is found in the way we love people who are different from us. The secret to learning how to love people in that way is in a simple, two-word phrase:

Draw near.

The parable of the good Samaritan is among the best known of all of Jesus' parables. Yet as often as I have read it and preached it, I did not recognize this one key word in this story until I read it this time around. It occurs in verse 34. After the Levite and priest had gone out of their way to avoid the poor beaten victim lying on the side of the road, a Samaritan—an outsider—approached the scene. Before he did any bandaging of any wounds, any application of oil, or transport to the inn, the very first thing that the Samaritan did was he "went to" the man (Luke 10:34).

The verb "go to" or "come to" or "draw near" in Greek is a very important one to Luke.

He uses that same verb when Jesus healed the hemorrhaging woman. It's the same verb used when Jesus fed the crowd and multiplied the food. It's the same verb that Luke used when Jesus healed the demon-possessed man. Over and over again, "drawing near" was the crucial first step toward true healing.

The key to loving others who are different from us is first to draw near to them.

This is hard. It happens so rarely. We are more prone to doing the opposite of drawing near to those who are different from us. We like to categorize and label, rather than look for commonality. We like to build walls instead of bridges.

In other words, our default position is to act like the Levites and priests in this story. When we see others who are different from us, we walk around them.

I once heard a sermon on the good Samaritan preached by Bart Campolo, the son of the famous author and speaker Tony Campolo. His lead question gripped my imagination. He asked, "Of all the characters in the good Samaritan story, who do you think Jesus would have identified with the most?" My quick and obvious conclusion was that, naturally, Jesus would have identified himself as the good Samaritan. He was the one to save poor, wretched souls like that man. He was the one with the compassionate heart. It was Jesus who loved the unlovable.

But wait a minute, Campolo said. Is it possible that, of all the characters in the story, the one Jesus would have identified with the most is the half-dead victim on the side of the road? After all, in another Gospel, Jesus identified with the hungry, the naked, the thirsty, the sick, and the imprisoned; for when we care for the least of these, we care for Jesus himself (Matthew 25:31-46).

There are two conclusions I drew from Campolo's interpretation. First, there is the unequivocal reminder that throughout the biblical narrative, God never sides with the bullies. God sides with the people being bullied. God is always identifying with the powerless, the beaten down, and the downcast—never with the proud and the bullish.

The second conclusion is just as important: when we draw near to the people who are different from us, when we look into their eyes and into their faces, we can see that not only are they no different from us, but we can also see Jesus himself.

They are made in the image of God, children of God just like us.

God, thank you for bridging the divide between you and me, through the work of Jesus. Help me to follow his example, that I might find his very image in people around me. Amen.

What difference would it make to see people who are different from you as children of God, just like you?

DAY 10

Luke 10:38-42

GOOFUS AND GALLANT

For a moment in Luke's Gospel, we might forget we are reading biblical literature and instead feel like we are reading a copy of *Highlights* magazine, catching the latest episode of *Goofus and Gallant*.

Maybe you are familiar with this cartoon. It's basically an ethics and morality lesson cloaked as a children's comic strip. On the left panel is a child named Goofus, who is usually up to something dangerous, impolite, or improper. "Goofus is running with scissors," "Goofus fails to say 'Please' and 'Thank You,'" or "Goofus doesn't share his toys."

On the right panel is Gallant, a well-kept, polite child who always does the right thing. "Gallant is walking with scissors pointing down," "Gallant is always respectful of adults," or "Gallant is always glad to share with others."

The premise, of course, is that there is a little bit of Goofus and Gallant in each of us, and those qualities are frequently at odds with each other. To follow the upright path, we must learn to suppress our inner Goofus and instead express our inner Gallant.

That's all well and good when it comes to obvious matters like carrying scissors and being polite. But, when it comes to spiritual matters like that which is expressed in this story of Mary and Martha, it is a more complex question altogether.

If we were to look at these two sisters objectively, we might have a hard time determining which one is Goofus and which one is Gallant. Martha, after all, does so many commendable things. She is the one who welcomes Jesus as a guest. She is the one who offers hospitality and serves him. There really ought to be nothing wrong with that, especially since the story just prior to this one is the parable of the good Samaritan in which the Samaritan is praised for showing hospitality to the victim and caring for his needs. Martha seems like the perfect poster child for that parable.

And, while Mary is praised for her attentiveness to Jesus' teaching, she is pretty much doing the same thing as her sister—giving Jesus her attention. It's just that they are doing so in very different ways.

So, which one is Goofus, and which one is Gallant?

Well, in Jesus' mind, apparently Martha is Goofus.

The exact reason for this conclusion, according to Jesus, is that Martha is "worried and distracted by many things," and has therefore forgotten that only "one thing is necessary." Mary has gotten it right, apparently, by choosing the "better part," and "it won't be taken away from her" (Luke 10:41-42).

But Jesus' response raises so many more questions. What is the one "necessary" thing? What is the better part? And what exactly is *it* that won't be taken away from Mary?

If Luke was really trying to craft a Goofus and Gallant cartoon, it doesn't seem at first like a very good one. It isn't immediately clear exactly what the lesson is here.

But maybe Luke gives us a clue by telling us what happens *after* the Mary and Martha story. In chapter 11, there is a series of passages about prayer. Verses 1 to 4 introduce the Lord's Prayer, which Jesus offers in response to a disciple's request, "Lord, teach us to pray." In verses 5 to 8, Jesus teaches the disciples a lesson on how to pray with persistence. And in verses 9 to 13, Jesus reminds the disciples that the God to whom they pray is a generous God who is ready to respond with good gifts.

What if the story of Mary and Martha is not a competing contrast between two different personalities, lifestyles, or work habits, the way we are accustomed to interpreting this story?

Instead, what if Mary and Martha set up two different ways to go about praying?

What if the "Martha" way to pray is with a distracted mind, and the "Mary" way to pray is through stillness and silence?

What if the "Martha" way to pray is by focusing more on the chaos of the moment, while the "Mary" way to pray is by losing yourself in the moment by focusing on the presence of God?

What if the "Martha" way to pray is to try to say and do the right things in order to get what you ask for, as if God were a vending machine that can grant your request if you push the right buttons? And what if the "Mary" way to pray is to acknowledge simply that God is God, and you are not?

What if the "Martha" way to pray is trying to get God to justify your anger and disappointment in others, but the "Mary" way to pray is being open to God's grace and its power to transform the way you see others?

Well, if that's true, then the answers to our questions become pretty clear:

What is the one thing that is "necessary"? It is a healthy and vital prayer life, which is the lifeblood of a follower of Jesus.

What is the "better part"? It is praying in a way that focuses on praise, gratitude, and obedience, rather than simply praying for God to bless you.

And what exactly is it that won't be taken away from Mary? It is the assurance that, through prayer, our sense of God's presence is strong no matter what happens in life.

So, which is it? Will you pray like Martha, or pray like Mary?

God, help me to simply be in your presence, offering you my undivided attention, my highest praise, and my fullest obedience. Amen.

In what way are you prone to pray like Martha? What can you start doing differently in order to pray like Mary?

DAY 11

Luke 11:1-13

THE WAY TO PRAY

The disciples were just like us. They knew the importance of prayer but needed to know the techniques. They wanted to know the best way to pray. The best time to pray.

They understood its purpose; now they wanted to know its practice. Luke points out directly what Matthew only implies:

The disciples asked Jesus how to pray.

Jesus' answer, of course, is the greatest prayer in Christian tradition. The Lord's Prayer is important not because it is a scripted formula that can be uttered like a magical incantation, but because it orients our lives toward God and recalibrates our priorities.

First, the prayer refocuses on God.

Hallowed be *your* name.

Your kingdom come.

Your will be done, on earth as it is in heaven.

Prayer puts us in our place and reminds us that we are not the center of the universe. God is the center of all of existence, and we are merely orbiting satellites. It is in the act of prayer that we become deeply connected to the source and strength of our lives.

In prayer, our hearts become infused with the heart of God, and our minds become transformed by the grace of God. We feel what God feels. We are moved by what moves God. We start to see our enemies not as objects of scorn, but as fellow children of God. We start to see the situations of people around the world not as distant headlines, but as a mission field ripe for the harvest. Slowly, as our prayers focus us more and more on God, our own problems become smaller, and the world becomes bigger. Our capacity to see the earth as the potential new home for the kingdom of God gets wider and wider and wider.

Prayer is all about God. It is about God's vision for a new earth and God's deep compassion for all human beings. It is about God's unimaginable capacity to create new life out of dying existence, new hope out of darkness. If you need hope for hopeless times, love for unlovable people, strength for draining circumstances, or a vision for a threatened world, prayer directs you toward the God who is the answer to all problems.

Second, the Lord's Prayer refocuses us on how we should change.

Give us this day our daily bread—free us from the belief that we can provide for our needs on our own. Forgive us, and help us to forgive other people. Help us to resist evil and temptation.

Prayer must not only focus on God; it must also change you. It is not just about asking for things to happen; but about asking for a change to happen within us, so that we can live the life we are meant to live.

If the first part of the prayer focuses us on God and challenges us to change our perspectives, the second part of the Lord's Prayer focuses on our individual lives and challenges us to change our behavior.

Prayer should influence your practice. It ought to shape your words, inform your actions, and dictate every step of your journey.

It's possible to forgive someone else, but if it's not done with a foundation of God-focused prayer, you won't change from it.

It's possible to fight temptation now and then. But unless it's done with prayer, you may win the battles, but you won't prevail in the war.

It's possible to have your needs met in your physical life. But unless those needs are met in prayer, you'll never fully acknowledge or thank the one who met those needs in your life.

When you pray, mean it. Believe it. Then, act as if that prayer makes a difference.

God, thank you for teaching me this prayer. Continue to teach me how to pray, so that I might live into the words of the Lord's Prayer rather than just recite its words. Amen.

Do you know the Lord's Prayer by heart? When have you ever recited it during a moment when it had deep significance to you?

DAY 12

John 7:53–8:11 (7:14–8:59)

TWO SIDES OF THE SAME SOUL

John 8 records the story of "the woman caught in adultery." At least that's the way the tale is commonly named. We are so captivated by sensationalized news these days that we don't even think about calling it the story of "the conniving religious authorities" or "the interruption at the temple."

No, our tendency is to skip right to the scandalous. There was a woman, and she had been caught cheating. Never mind the fact that it takes two people to commit such a deed. Never mind that adultery wasn't the only sin forbidden in Hebrew law and punishable by death. The spotlight was clearly on this woman, even though, in the grand scheme of things, she was a mere pawn in a high-stakes power play between the religious establishment and the Son of God.

For a moment, I'd like for you to imagine the eyes and faces of the main characters. First, there were the legal experts and the Pharisees. They were the keepers of the law, the ethical code enforcers, the ones ready to blow the whistle at the slightest violation. Imagine the smugness on their faces, the steel in their gaze, the look of triumph in their eyes. They had concocted the perfect set-up to bring down the upstart from Nazareth, even if it did require a little finagling and framing to make it happen.

John makes it very clear that this woman was *"caught in adultery"* (John 8:3-4, italics added) As in, caught right in the middle of the act. I'm not sure how that happens, except that there had to be a lot of spying, waiting, and watching. In other words, her being caught was likely not incidental. The Pharisees were ready to catch her, just waiting for her to walk into their trap.

We might also imagine the look on the woman's face. Sheer dread. Terror. Eyes sullen, head bowed, body trembling. It's one thing to be caught in the act of sinning. It's even worse to be dragged into the public eye, before the court of public opinion, under the scornful glare of so many people casting judgment upon you. Eyeballs feel like laser beams, and your heart beats like a steel drum. To make things even worse, you feel like an unwilling rope in a tug-of-war between two religious titans. It's the last place you want to be, for the last reason on earth you want to be there. She probably felt shame, mixed with anger, mixed with terror. It's the worst combination of emotions.

If I were to write the headline of this story, it would not be "Woman Caught in Adultery" or "Interruption at the Temple." I would be torn between two options. The first might be "Two Sides of the Same Soul." That's because John portrays both the Pharisees and this poor woman with such vividness that it's hard not to identify with both of them. If you want to imagine what either of them looked like, all you have to do is look in the mirror. You've made those same faces before and had the same look in your eyes.

We are as equally capable of being the condemned as we are of being the condemner. We have all done things we wish we could take back, and we have all been among the first to notice others when they do the same. We have felt the shame, and we have imparted the judgment. Their looks are our looks. Sometimes, we feel both at the same time.

Yes, it is true that the woman was *caught* doing something she shouldn't have done. But the more we think about the story, we are the ones, in fact, who are caught. We are caught between being the Pharisees and the woman, even simultaneously.

That puts Jesus front and center, of course, to settle this dispute within our souls. This story becomes less about how Jesus is going to wiggle out of this clever little trap, and more about how Jesus is going to lead us out of the trap we find ourselves in.

And what does he do? He stoops down and writes in the dirt.

That's what my other headline would be: "What Did He Write?" We're not told what he scribbled. We don't know if it was words, or a picture, or simple kinesthetic doodling. Maybe he was just bending down to think as he sketched. We don't have any idea.

But we do know that he did it twice.

The first time was in response to the Pharisees' questioning (John 8:5) where they questioned, "What are you going to do, Jesus? Follow Moses' law, or let this woman off the hook?" The more he scribbled, the more he pressed. While we don't have any idea what he wrote, we do know what he eventually said: "Whoever hasn't sinned should throw the first stone" (8:7).

That was enough to stop the Pharisees dead in their tracks. They had posed a binary choice: guilty or not guilty, life or death, freedom or punishment. But Jesus changed the premise of the question entirely, making it not about adherence to the law but about the condition of their souls. He made it less about others' sins and more about their own. We have no idea what he wrote on the ground, but his conclusion was pretty clear:

Who are you to judge?

That should have been the end of the story. The trap was not sprung, Jesus had slipped out of their hands, and he taught them a valuable lesson. But there was still the other party to address, the other side of the story, the other side of the soul, to redeem.

Jesus doesn't just want to redeem the part of us that refuses to see our sin and takes it out on others. He also wants to redeem the part of us that knows our sin all too well and takes it out on ourselves. Both are important to Jesus.

So, he scribbles again, and this time stops to address the woman (John 8:8-11). It is here that we receive one of the most poignant, tender, and powerful exchanges in the entire Gospel.

Jesus stood up and said to her, "Woman, where are they? Is there no one to condemn you?"

She said, "No one, sir."

Jesus said, "Neither do I condemn you. Go, and from now on, don't sin anymore."

(John 8:10-11)

For all we know, this was the only time Jesus ever scribbled in the dirt. But I'd like to think that in the act of touching the ground at that moment, he found himself grounded. That same dirt and dust he touched with his finger was the very same earth God used to create his own body. He was fully human, and he knew it. He was susceptible to the very same temptations that both the Pharisees and this woman faced. And maybe, by touching the dirt, he empathized with the utter frailties of both of them.

In the process of doing so, he remembered something that they had forgotten. God loved them both. And so would he. He would love them enough to meet them where they are, and he would love them too much to leave them there, as the old saying about grace goes.

Here's the best news of all: Jesus loves you the same way, no matter how much you are like the Pharisees, or like the woman, or even both at the same time.

God, thank you for your amazing grace. Forgive me for the ways I have fallen short of your best intentions for me and for the ways I have judged others. Lead me to become more like Jesus every day. Amen.

Which character do you identify with the most in this story? When have you ever been like the Pharisees? When have you been like the woman?

DAY 13

John 9:1-7 (9:1-41)

BEYOND CAUSE AND EFFECT

The disciples come to Jesus with a question that captures one of the greatest barriers people have in the Christian faith. It is the question of the nature of suffering and evil, and of God's relationship to them. On the surface, the question they pose is a straightforward one: upon seeing a man who had been blind since birth, they ask Jesus whether it was the man's or his parents' sin that caused his condition.

In the disciples' minds, as in ours, suffering and evil must have a *cause*. We are hesitant to chalk up tragedy to chance, for we want to believe we are somewhat protected from having to go through tough times and that if we will simply do the right things, we can avoid them.

In other words, we want to believe that the world is built on a framework of cause and effect, and that people can avoid bad situations if they can simply avoid causing them to begin with. The disciples' question poses a false choice, of course, because we know that not all suffering is caused by our own actions, just like always doing the right thing does not preclude us from suffering.

Professor of preaching Tom Long has called this problem "The Impossible Chess Match." On the one side is all we have believed or at least wanted to believe about God's love and power. On the other side is the reality of a world where innocent people suffer and evil exists. The two sides are at war, in a game never to be fully resolved.[1]

There is, even in the Bible, a similar chess match going on, between two theological perspectives, with neither of them winning. Smack dab in the middle of our Old Testament, in the Hebrew Bible, is a section we often refer to as the Wisdom Literature: Job, Proverbs, and Ecclesiastes. They are commonly known as the Wisdom Literature (which also includes some of the Psalms), and they are in the Bible for a fascinating reason.

Right in the middle of all the stories about exodus and exile, obedience and punishment, justice and injustice, faithfulness and unfaithfulness, these books offer commentary on God's relationship to hardship.

On the one side, you have Psalms and Proverbs, verses like "[the wicked] are like dust that the wind blows away" (Psalm 1:4), "God will shatter the heads of his enemies" (Psalm 68:21), "Surely goodness and mercy shall follow me / all the days of my life" (Psalm 23:6 NRSV), "Trust in the LORD with all your heartheart, / ...and he will keep your ways straight" (Proverbs 3:5-6), and "Let your heart guard my commands / because they will help you live a long time / and provide you with well-being" (Proverbs 3:1-2). They convey the message: trust God, follow God. God is faithful, God is just, and all will work out in the end.

We like these verses. This is our kind of God.

On the other side of the argument is Job and Ecclesiastes. There's a story about a man who suffered great injustice for no rational reason (Job). And there's a teacher on a quest for the meaning of life, with no conclusion except to say that life is just meaningless, a wisp of air, a breath, and then it's gone: "Vanity of vanities! All is vanity" (Ecclesiastes 1:2 NRSV).

In the story of the blind man, the disciples are clearly approaching the man's blindness from the perspective of Psalms and Proverbs. They believe that his suffering must have had a cause and that it could have been avoided.

But notice that Jesus' rebuke of the disciples' assumption does not mean he agrees with Job and Ecclesiastes. Jesus is not willing to swing the pendulum entirely the other way, to simply say that the man's blindness was a random, haphazard event of chance.

In fact, Jesus wishes to transcend the binary choice entirely, not by focusing on the suffering but by focusing on God. He cares less about what *caused* the suffering, and more about *what God can do* in the midst of it. During our toughest times, God's power, presence, and grace can be revealed. Jesus is right there with us: "While I am in the world, I am the light of the world" (John 9:5).

In the end, the man was not just healed of his blindness; he was healed in his spirit. He came to a saving belief in Jesus, and subsequently worshiped him.

You may be going through a very difficult time right now as you struggle to embrace the uncertainty of your own life. You may have wondered what you did to cause it and if it could have been avoided. That may or may not be the case. But this story reminds us that the cause of your suffering is not the biggest question. Instead, the biggest question is how God can be revealed in it. How can you come to see the power and love of God in the midst of your situation? How might it lead you to a deeper belief in Jesus and a more earnest worship of God?

God, thank you for not leaving me alone in the midst of my difficulties. Thank you for Jesus, who is the light in the midst of my darkness. Help me to see you and trust in you, even amid my suffering. Amen.

When have you struggled over the nature of suffering and evil in your life and in the world? How might you begin to look for God's presence and power in the midst of your suffering?

---

1 Thomas G. Long, *What Shall We Say? Evil, Suffering, and the Crisis of Faith* (Grand Rapids: Eerdmans, 2011), 25.

DAY 14
John 10:11-21 (10:1-42)
THE BETTER-THAN-GOOD SHEPHERD

Shepherds are among the Bible's favorite people. Abel, Lot, Jacob, Jacob's sons—they were all shepherds. Moses became one while on the run, before he came across the burning bush. David was a singing shepherd before he became king. Then there were the wonderful Bethlehem shepherds, the first to hear the news about Christ's birth.

The Bible loves shepherds.

The Bible may even love shepherds more than biblical people did. They were often lower-class citizens, several rungs lower in notoriety than the noble class of patricians and public officials in the Roman empire. They were not learned religious scholars or priests. To be a shepherd warranted no fame or glory.

For Jesus to name himself the Good Shepherd would have been a total shock to John's audience. Jesus was, in effect, saying that he was willing to associate with the lowly of society. Just as he often did throughout his ministry, Jesus took conventional wisdom and flipped it on its ear.

Here's one more reversal. Shepherds eventually sacrificed their sheep. They provided the means through which people could make their blood offerings in the temple and restore their relationship with God. Without the shepherds, there would be no sheep, no means to sacrifice, and ultimately, no relationship with God.

That's why the most shocking thing Jesus said in identifying himself as the Good Shepherd is this: "I give up my life for the sheep" (John 10:15).

This Good Shepherd was not in the business of leading his sheep to slaughter but saving his sheep from slaughter. He wasn't going to allow them to die but was going to die in their place. This was the greatest, most radical reversal of all: the shepherd is sacrificed, not the sheep. What a reversal!

Of course, if Jesus is the Shepherd, that makes us the sheep. At first, being called sheep may seem like an insult. We often have disparaging images of sheep as dim-witted, bumbling, and prone to wandering. And as accurate as that may be in the way it describes us at times, it doesn't seem like a very endearing self-image. But when Jesus described the life of a shepherd in this Gospel reading from John, we get some insight into what being a sheep really meant.

"My sheep listen to my voice," Jesus says in John 10:27. "I know them and they follow me." Jesus says that it is not only acceptable, but compulsory, for us to be like sheep, for sheep know the voice of the shepherd. The relationship between shepherd and sheep is one of familiarity, which means that Jesus knows us fully and deeply. You are not a random combination of protein and water, taking up space on the planet, with no meaning in life. You are a person with a purpose, known intimately by the Jesus who not only created you, but who has offered his own life for you. Your only task is to be led by that shepherd to green pastures, to still waters, and in paths of righteousness.

You may feel dim-witted, bumbling, and prone to wandering. But Jesus knows you intimately, and gives you the very same command that he gave to his disciples and that he gives to all of us: "Follow me."

God, thank you for knowing me fully. In you, I find my truest purpose and meaning. Teach me to follow you. Amen.

In what ways are you struggling to hear God's voice today? What changes can you make in the way you listen to God and mute all the other voices in your world?

DAY 15

John 11:47-54

THE CENTRAL CONFLICT

Good screenwriters and novelists know the secret to any good story. It's not just about compelling characters, a vivid setting, or beautiful language. For a story to be really gripping, you need conflict. There must be some struggle between two opposing forces, with no clear indication of the resolution.

The Gospel writers each knew this, and John chose to get right to the heart of the struggle here in chapter 11. The chief priests and Pharisees, the antagonists in the Gospel story, have had quite enough of Jesus, and in this passage, John tells us why: "What are we going to do? This man is doing many miraculous signs! If we let him go on like this, everyone will believe in him. Then the Romans will come and take away both our temple and our people" (John 11:47-48).

In other words, the religious officials see Jesus as nothing less than a threat to the status quo and to their normal way of living. They had carved out a clear livelihood for themselves, based on a way of thinking, behaving, and relating to others. As long as they could use the Hebrew Scriptures as a hammer, they could see in the world nothing but nails. But when Jesus came along, he offered a very different way of seeing the world—not as one full of nails, but of possibilities of grace and forgiveness. When people started to believe it, the religious leaders saw Jesus as a threat.

The temptation, of course, is to villainize the chief priests and the Pharisees. It's fun to do because in some ways, it gets us off the hook. As long as we can find religious hypocrisy in other people, then we can insulate ourselves from finding the same within us.

But that may not be what John is inviting us to do. What if we admit that there is a little bit of high-brow, Pharisaic hypocrisy inside ourselves? What if we discover that there are parts of our lives that aren't quite right but have settled into a kind of status quo that we have grown accustomed to? What if we are reluctant to hear the challenging, compelling words of Jesus because of just how disruptive they might be to our own preferred ways of thinking and acting?

In other words, what if we discover that the central conflict is not in the story, but in our own souls?

On the other side of the struggle in the story is Caiaphas, the high priest that year. He tried to be the voice of belief and the voice of reason. "Haven't you all been paying attention?" he said to the others, in a manner of speaking. "He told us he would die so that everyone might live. You know as well as I do that Jesus is coming to promise new life. But in order for that to happen, old ways have to die. Don't you all see? Don't you all get it?"

Don't you and I?

Of course we don't. That's not our normal mode of operation. We are wired for self-preservation and self-advancement. We strive to avoid death, not embrace it. We try live our life to the fullest, not to lose it. And when something—or someone—comes along and challenges us, ... well, that's hard to take in. We'd rather ignore it. Or worse.

It's the "or worse" that the religious officials decided to do.

There would be no turning back now for Jesus, and he knew it. From this moment on, he recognized that there would be a target on his back, and the religious establishment was dead set on putting him away. He would choose to avoid them the best he could for the time being. It wasn't because he was afraid. And it wasn't because he was trying to run away. It simply was not yet the right time. There were still a few more things to do, more pieces to fall together.

When the time was right, all would be revealed.

Jesus knew something that the chief priests and Pharisees didn't. They might have meant him harm, but they were actually acting according to the plan. They weren't adversaries after all but accomplices in the greatest miracle the world would ever see. This conflict between Caiaphas and the Pharisees wasn't a conflict at all, in

God's eyes. Resurrection would soon be upon them, and that would change everything. New life and new possibility would burst into the picture, and nothing would ever be the same.

God, I acknowledge that there are many parts of my life that feel set in their ways. Forgive me for seeing you as a threat. Help me to be open to your transforming power, your steadfast love, and your overwhelming grace. Amen.

In what way can you identify with the chief priests and the Pharisees? What parts of your life fall short of God's ideal for you yet are part of your comfortable pattern of living?

DAY 16

Luke 13:10-17

WHEN JESUS DOES THE CALLING

Jesus healed a lot of people in the Gospels. But there is something different about this miracle story. Maybe it has something to do with the way it begins. In other stories, the build-up to the miracle is as interesting as the miracle itself. When he healed the blind man in Mark 10, Jesus first asked him, "What do you want me to do for you?" and made the man name his need before Jesus would help him (Mark 10:51). In other stories, the person who needed healing came to Jesus begging and pleading, like the father of the demon-possessed boy in Mark 9:21-24 or the Canaanite woman in Matthew 15:21-28. And then there was the woman dealing with the lifelong hemorrhage, who not only approached Jesus, but touched him without words, experiencing instant healing from her condition (Mark 5:25-34).

In other words, in most other healing stories, there is an interaction, an approach, or a plea for help. There is a major set-up before the miraculous surprise.

Not in this story. What's fascinating about this woman is that there is no such interaction beforehand. She doesn't approach him. She does no begging for his attention. She probably couldn't even look him in the eye if she wanted to, given her sad condition of having to stare at the ground bent over for the better part of the last eighteen years.

That's what happens when you are perpetually hunched over. You can't look forward, and you can't look up. You're stuck looking down, at your feet, staring at your present steps, not able to look ahead into the future, to dream about where to go next.

That's not only true physically; it's also true of living with a hunched-over spirit. It's the kind of condition that leads one to isolation and hopelessness, despair and sadness. It's what makes you want to sit in the corner of a dark room and stop wondering if the light is ever going to come back on. Your eyes are too adjusted to the darkness, and you've stopped believing that things are ever going to change.

This woman was not going to be approaching Jesus for help. It's not necessarily because she didn't want to but because she forgot how to and because she didn't think she could, even if she did want to.

That's why Jesus did the calling.

He called her over to him, which itself had to have been a foreign sound in this woman's ears. All she had likely been hearing until then were jeers of derision or whispers of empathy. She wasn't someone people called over. She was someone people overlooked. Or worse, felt sorry for. But that's not what Jesus did. He caught her attention, and said to her, "Hi. Can you come over here for a minute?"

Already, right then and there, it was a miracle in the making.

Jesus didn't ask her any questions. He didn't require her to speak, didn't demand that she beg and plead. For other miracle recipients, there may have been an application process, a period of testing and evaluation in Jesus' mind. But not here. For this woman, this woeful, desperate, and isolated woman, Jesus had seen all he needed to see.

And he said to her, "Woman, you are set free from your sickness" (Luke 13:12). Then he went one step further. He took his hands and raised her up (13:13). The fingers of the very God who formed her from the dust took her wayward spine and made it true, took her awkward musculature and made it healthy, took her downward gaze and pointed it straight ahead again.

For the first time in a long, long time, she could look someone in the eyes again. What she saw were the eyes of her savior.

There is much about this woman that you might identify with today. You know her feelings of abandonment and loss, and you, too, know what it's like to live in a perpetual downward gaze. The thought of asking God or anyone else for help seems utterly useless. It's not because you don't believe in God but because you don't believe it would do any good.

If that's you today, then there's good news for you. God already sees you. God is calling you over.

It's not to say the healing will be instantaneous, like it was for this woman. It might take time. Frankly, it likely will. It may create other problems you weren't expecting. That's certainly what happened when the synagogue leader saw the woman's healing, which happened on the sabbath. Others might not understand. Others might not expect it. Others may wish that you would go back to the way you were before. Sometimes, healing is disruptive.

But take heart. At the end of the day, what you will still have is a God who sees you, who looks you in the eye, who raises you up, and faces you forward.

Then you can see the brighter days that are ahead.

God, thank you for seeing me, even when I feel that no one else notices me. Thank you for calling me and for offering healing to my mind, body, and spirit. Amen.

In what ways is Jesus calling you to come over to him? What do you think Jesus is trying to tell you?

DAY 17

Luke 13:18-35

THE FOX AND THE HEN

Let's see if we can get this straight. The Pharisees come to Jesus "concerned for his safety." Yeah, right. That's like the Joker caring about Batman, or Lex Luthor worried that Superman might find Kryptonite.

But it's true. These everyday enemies of Jesus came to him and said, "Go! Get away from here, because Herod wants to kill you" (Luke 13:31). When Jesus responded to the Pharisees' feigned concern over his safety, we can almost hear Jesus say, "What, do you think I was born yesterday?"

We cannot be sure of their motives, but we can reasonably assume that they were being disingenuous. He knew they didn't have his best interest at heart. In fact, he was so wise to their little trick and their alliance with Herod that he called Herod a "fox"—a creature with a reputation for being sly and conniving.

Jesus is savvy enough to know what's most important in life and what are mere distractions. That's what a lot of interpersonal conflict is in your life, anyway. Distractions. Such conflicts are roads that steer you away from the things that ought to be your top priorities: family, career, and doing God's will. Any kind of conflict that steers you off those main highways is a distraction.

Jesus brushes aside that trap and immediately focuses on what matters most to him: Jerusalem. Now, Jerusalem was more than just the center of the people's political, theological, and social order. It was also Jesus' ultimate destination, the culmination of his earthly mission to redeem the world and rectify people's broken relationships with God. To Jesus, nothing else mattered. Jesus knew that there was only one thing he needed to focus on, one priority that was most important:

healing broken relationships between humans and each other, and between humans and God.

It is interesting that this is the only Gospel to record this exchange with the Pharisees, including Jesus' description of Herod as a fox. Luke offers a lesson here for anyone suffering the scorn of opponents: stick to the mission. Remember what's most important. Jesus refused to get hung up on the feeble power games played by his political enemies, and chose instead to get to work and accomplish the tasks he was called to fulfill.

Having made his point, Luke could have concluded the story here, with a determined Jesus focused on his mission. Instead, he complements this portrait with a depiction of an emotional, poignant Jesus. In contrast to the fox, we see Jesus as the hen, and we can hear the ache in his voice as he longs for the people to turn from their waywardness and turn toward this new kingdom.

> *Jerusalem, Jerusalem, you who kill the prophets and stone those who were sent to you! How often have I wanted to gather your people just as a hen gathers her chicks under her wings. But you didn't want that.*
>
> (Luke 13:34)

That is such a different picture of Jesus, isn't it? He isn't one who is just wise or strong, but one who is devastated and compassionate. He desperately, desperately, wants the people of Jerusalem—the people of God—to figure out that what they are doing is harmful, unhealthy, and unholy. But they just can't seem to get it.

This is a side of Jesus that so many of us can relate to. It's like the parents who want desperately for their children to make the right decisions but know that they cannot control their children's choices. It's like the married couple who has fallen out of love with each other, trying to figure out how to make things work, knowing that they cannot control each other's reactions, emotions, or choices.

It's like God, the presence of love and goodness throughout all creation, who constantly yearns, desires, and persuades the world to make choices toward harmony and beauty rather than chaos and harm. Yet God knows that because of our free will, we are always free to choose against God. Love is only love when you choose to give it and choose to receive it. Otherwise, it's coercion, deception, and abuse. We aren't forced to love God or to love one another.

That's what was happening in the heart of Jesus in this passage. This is a portrait of a longing, perhaps tearful Jesus, who had to acknowledge that though he was empowered with the capacity to perform miracles, even raise people from the dead, the one thing he could not do—the one thing he chose not to do—was force people to love.

God, thank you for loving me as a hen loves her young. Empower me to live and love as you have called me and help me to stick to the mission of what you want me to do.

What conflicts in your life might be considered mere distractions from what is most important? How might you go about resolving those conflicts, in order to stick to the mission of what God wants you to do?

DAY 18

Luke 14:1-11 (14:1-35)

TRUE HUMILITY

Here's what I wonder at the outset of Luke 14. The chapter begins with Jesus sharing a meal in the home of a prominent Pharisee, a member of a group who were the consistent antagonists to Jesus throughout the Gospels.

So, I wonder, how did that invitation go?

Did Jesus invite himself over, much like he did with Zacchaeus, the tax collector? Did he tell the Pharisee, "Put some extra water in the soup and pull up another chair at the table. Tonight, I am dining at your house"? Or was it the Pharisee who made the first move? If that's the case, I can only imagine the fierce pushback he must have gotten from the other religious leaders. ("What are you doing? How could you invite *Jesus* over for a meal? He's a threat to everything we believe in and stand for! How *could* you?")

The truth is, we don't know how that initial invitation came about, and Luke doesn't think it important enough to tell us. But given our current culture, when our society is so deeply polarized and entrenched in our own ideological tribes and factions, I think it is worth something that even Jesus and this Pharisee—not even any old Pharisee, but a *leader* of Pharisees—found a way to sit down and break bread together. That alone is a good example for us to follow.

There is more to the story, of course, for Jesus notices something once the dinner begins. Other invited guests start lunging for the prominent seats right next to this influential Pharisee. Like politicians campaigning for a cabinet post or fans clamoring for a selfie with a celebrity, these guests are all jockeying for the prized seat next to the master of the house.

As Jesus watches this scene unfold, he stops the dinner in its tracks and decides to start preaching. The point of his message is basically this: if you clamor for the top, you will be sent to the bottom. But if you humbly begin at the bottom, then others will elevate you to prominence.

I'm not sure that Jesus was literally instructing the guests on banquet etiquette or polite manners at dinner parties. But he was certainly trying to get his audience to adopt a position of humility in every aspect of their lives.

When I was growing up, I had a pretty distorted view of what it meant to be humble. I thought to be humble meant you thought of yourself as pretty lowly. It meant minimizing my own talents and abilities, not being proud of who I was or what I was able to do. It meant that I had to think of everyone else as better than I was. For me, humility was the exact opposite of boasting. Rather than seeing myself as everything, I thought of myself as nothing.

I don't know if that meshes with your view of humility, but that is neither healthy nor biblical. Humility does not mean seeing yourself as nothing. It is not to be equated with low self-esteem.

Instead, look at the word *humility* a little more closely. It comes from the Latin word *humus*, which literally means "dirt." Humility does not mean seeing ourselves as dirt, but it does mean seeing ourselves as *grounded*. Earthy. No better and no worse than the rest of all creation.

It means acknowledging that you are connected to every other living creature on earth, and you are as dependent on others as they are on you. You cannot claim to be better than anyone else, because you depend on others. And you are no worse than anyone else, because others depend on you.

Here's another way of looking at it. You are never as bad as you think you are, and you are never as good as other people might say you are. In other words, the appropriate balance between ego and self-abasement is always remembering that your value is found neither in what you think of yourself or dependent on the affirmation that people give you.

The converse is true, also. You are never as good as you think you are, and you are never as bad as others might say you are. True humility is the gift of seeing yourself the way God sees you, and seeing yourself as part of an interconnected dependence on the lives of people with you and around you.

God, thank you for humbling yourself in Jesus, who took the form of a human being to give himself to the world. Help me to do the same for others. Amen.

Think about the fact that Jesus and a leader of the Pharisees had dinner together. How might that encourage you to build bridges of common understanding with someone with whom you disagree?

DAY 19

Luke 15:11-32 (15:1–16:18)

UNUSUAL, UNCONDITIONAL LOVE

In the story commonly known as the Prodigal Son, consider what the younger son was asking of his father. Our childlike interpretation would render his request simply an advance on his inheritance. But it was much more than that.

According to noted biblical scholar Kenneth Bailey, in the ancient Near East, to make such a request essentially meant that the younger son wished for his father to be dead. Because they were living in a village that was agriculturally based, the younger son's request to sell his portion of the land and leave with the profits was tantamount to saying that he wanted nothing more to do with both his father and his whole village. This was a scandal of headline proportions. The hearers of this parable in Jesus' day would have been shocked by the audacity of this brash young man who seemed to wish for his father's death and wanted to be torn out of the fabric of his community.[1]

This may be a difficult part of the story to relate to, but consider that in the darkest days of life, you may have experienced a God who felt dead to you, a time when faith was inconsequential and where you were no longer part of a community of love and support. You might think having such feelings of doubt and disillusionment in your faith makes you unworthy of being a Christian, but you ought to know that you are not alone.

It doesn't take long for a person in such darkness to identify with what happens next. The younger son then took that inheritance and squandered his money on riotous living. His entire life fell apart. He lost his mind, his faculties, his moral compass: nothing was left in him or about him that even remotely resembled a fully integrated person. He had destroyed himself.

And so, out of nothing more than sheer desperation for three square meals and shelter at night, the young son decided to take a turn homeward. He knew what that meant. He was sure to face the scorn of a village that was still angry over his departure, to say nothing of his father's likely response.

That is why it is so astonishing to hear what the father did when he saw his son coming toward him from a distance. First, he ran toward him. Perhaps, as Bailey notes, this is noteworthy because in order to run in those days, he would have had to hike up his tunic to free his legs and run quickly. And in those days, exposing your bare legs was to bring embarrassment to yourself. But the father didn't care. He was willing to bring public embarrassment upon himself for the sake of his son.

Perhaps the father was running in order to meet his son before he got to the border of the village, before the son was greeted by anger and distrust once people saw him coming and recognized who he was. Quite literally, the father was laying down his own reputation in order to welcome his son home.

There in the midst of the most beautiful embrace in the Bible, the young man realizes the unconditional love that his father had shown him, seeks his forgiveness, and is welcomed back into the family.

Here is what the Prodigal Son story tells you today: God's unconditional love for you is not contingent on your ability to understand it. You don't have to comprehend it in order for it to be a reality in your life.

God's love is unusual because we don't expect it, and it's unconditional because we don't deserve it. Just when you turn around to repent of your sins, you discover that God has been running toward you the whole time, eager to embrace you and say, "Welcome home."

What's more, God's unconditional love for you gives you the ability to reconcile your relationships with other people with whom you are in a broken relationship. That, after all, is the final act of this story. After the father threw a party, complete with the choicest of foods, and the gifts of sandals, a ring, and a robe, the elder brother comes in. The dutiful, obedient, rule-abiding son enters, and we discover just how much like him we really are.

Forgiveness doesn't make sense. Unconditional love is completely irrational. It doesn't fit into our ideas for justice and consequences and punishment. But that is the way God loves us. That is the way we can love each other so that we can say to one another, with open arms and genuine love: "Welcome home."

God, thank you for loving me unconditionally, even when I don't understand it or deserve it. Help me love others in the same way. Amen.

Is there anything about God's love for you that you find too hard to understand, accept, or believe? What can help you grow in your appreciation of God's love?

---

1 Kenneth E. Bailey, "The Pursuing Father" *Christianity Today*, October 26, 1998; http://www.christianitytoday.com/ct/1998/october26/8tc034.html?start=1. Accessed September 7, 2017

DAY 20

Luke 16:19-31

THE PARABLE OF THE FIVE BROTHERS

So, what do we make of the story of the rich man and Lazarus?

On one level, we might see this as a story about heaven and hell. The imagery here is much too vivid to ignore, and it feeds some of our popular notions of what heaven and hell will be like. The rich man is sent down there for punishment, based on criteria that are neither fully revealed nor critically important to the story. All we really know is that he was sentenced to a place of torment, in a place that was really hot. It's enough to convince us that it's a place we really don't want to be.

Lazarus, on the other hand, winds up in a much better place, carried by angels into the presence of the great patriarch Abraham. The word *heaven* is not used per se, but we know enough to conclude that it's a place we'd much rather be, particularly for eternity.

Nonetheless, I'm not sure that the reason Jesus tells the story is to give us a glimpse of heaven and hell.

What if this were a story about the dichotomy between the rich and the poor? That would certainly be in keeping with the overall theme of Luke, who consistently favors the marginalized and the oppressed throughout his Gospel. It comes on the heels of Jesus telling the disciples that they cannot serve God and money (Luke 16:13). It is a story of reversals, in which the rich on earth are sent to eternal punishment while the poor on earth are given reward, and the chasm between the two is wide. It wouldn't take too much of a leap to connect this story to the disparity between the rich and the poor in our societies, and God's command for us to use the richness of our means to help those who are destitute among us.

Fair enough. But I'm not sure this story is all about economic disparity either.

In fact, I don't think that either the rich man or Lazarus is our main point of connection into the story. I don't think Luke is inviting us to connect with either of them, but rather with a group of people we aren't introduced to until the very end of the story, in verse 28: "I beg you, Father, send Lazarus to my father's house. I have five brothers. He needs to warn them so that they don't come to this place of agony" (Luke 16:27-28). Abraham refuses to send Lazarus, though, because they have already been sent Moses and the prophets. What if the characters we are to identify with the most are not the rich man or Lazarus, but the people who are still alive on earth: Lazarus's five brothers? What would it take for you and me—the five brothers in the story—to believe in the possibility of eternity with God, and to claim that promise with certainty and conviction?

Those five brothers may represent the myriad of reasons people are reluctant to believe in the good news of Jesus. Maybe one brother had been scarred by a bad experience in a prior faith community. Maybe he's still thinking about the hypocrisy, the condescension, the feeling of being ostracized.

Maybe another brother was struggling with the relationship between faith and reason, and saw the two as incompatible. Maybe he was just looking for some evidence, some proof, that these religious convictions had any truth to them.

Maybe another brother was in the midst of deep pain and grief. He was walking through a dark time in life, and the suffering was so suffocating he was just trying to focus on making it through each day. He couldn't begin to think about eternity. One day at a time, step by step.

Maybe another brother was just like his deceased rich brother. He had the world at his fingertips, able to do anything, buy anything, and become anything he wanted, with power, prestige, and money to spare. Or so he thought.

Maybe the fifth brother is not even in the picture. He's all alone, with no connections to his family, or to anyone else for that matter. No one has really talked to him in a long time, and for all they know, he's out there somewhere, lost.

I don't know why Luke says there were *five* brothers. The truth is, if we added up all the reasons lots of people are reluctant to believe in the promise of God's love and salvation, then the number could be many times that.

So, the question is, if you were one of those brothers, what would it take for you to believe?

I don't mean just believe with your mind, of course. I mean believing with a full-throated, gung-ho, all-in kind of commitment, in which you shed your apprehension and decide to follow Jesus with every aspect of your being.

What would it take?

Granted, we might find fault with Abraham's final conclusion. He said that not even someone coming back from the dead would be sufficient evidence to convince the most ardent skeptics. We would disagree, of course. Today, if someone were to come back from the dead and tell us everything about heaven, our ears would perk up and we would certainly listen.

But maybe that's Luke's point. That's what Jesus did two thousand years ago. And even if there is a part of us that has trouble believing in the Resurrection, there is still plenty of proof of the Resurrection today.

There are people who were spiraling downward with each passing breath into their hellish conditions, including addictions, resentment, guilt, longing, shame, and darkness of every sort you can name. Because of Jesus, they have been brought back to life. They have been resurrected to new hope and new possibility. You may know those people. They are in our churches, in our towns, and in many of our neighborhoods. You may even be one of them.

And, boy, do they have a story to tell. Will you believe it?

God, thank you for raising Jesus from the dead, and for continuing the work of resurrection in our lives. Help me offer the fullness of who I am into your transforming love, and help me believe in you. Amen.

What is your idea of heaven and hell? How important is it for you to have certainty about what will happen after you die?

DAY 21
Luke 17:1-10
FORGIVENESS AND FAITH

The disciples make many requests of Jesus throughout the Gospels. They ask him to feed a hungry crowd. They ask him to designate which of them is the greatest. They ask him to teach them how to pray. But it's this request in Luke 17 that may be the most earnest, the most heartfelt, and the most resonant with your faith today: "The apostles said to the Lord, 'Increase our faith!'" (Luke 17:5).

It's not that they didn't have any faith; it's that they didn't have enough. It's not that they didn't believe in Jesus at all; it's that the little belief they had in him was not enough to address the big concerns of life.

What was the presenting problem that prompted the disciples to realize their faith was woefully inadequate to the task? Forgiveness.

Luke begins the scene with Jesus talking to his disciples about their relationships with others. He warns them about causing others to stumble, telling them that doing so warrants a drastic fate with a large stone dropped into a lake. He's speaking in hyperbole, of course; there is no Hebrew law stipulating that such grievances are punishable by death in such means. But he is fully communicating the gravity of causing others to sin, and the disciples most assuredly took notice. But he's not done. To make things more difficult, Jesus then reminds the disciples that when others caused them offense, there was one and only one suitable response: forgiveness. To offer forgiveness to others for the wrongs done to you is a nonnegotiable facet of the Christian life. Not forgiving someone is simply not an option.

That's what prompts the disciples to say to Jesus, in what was likely sheer desperation, "Increase our faith!"

It is interesting that Luke would link forgiveness with faith. Those two don't usually go together in our minds. We think forgiveness is primarily an act of the will. We can choose to hold a grudge, let go of past hurts, or seek revenge. It is true that forgiveness requires intentionality and follow-through because it often goes against our basic instincts.

But according to Luke, forgiveness is not just an action or an intention. It is also a demonstration of faith. Embedded in the act of forgiveness is a conviction, not warranted by evidence or proof, that forgiving a person is the right thing to do in the long run. It may not be easy to do so (in fact it may feel next to impossible). It may not make any sense at all to ourselves or others. But at that place where reason and sensibility hit their limit, faith is there to carry us through the tender and fragile wake of our past hurts. To forgive with faith is to admit that this is hard work, but with God's help, it is possible.

Now consider this connection between forgiveness and faith as we approach the rest of this Scripture passage. For when it comes to the parable of the mustard seed, we discover that our ability to speak a tree out of its roots and a mountain into the sea is not about being able to maneuver material objects like a Jedi from *Star Wars*. Instead, this is about being able to accomplish the difficult work of forgiveness, and to perform the impossible task of living a holy and righteous life.

In other words, having the faith of a mustard seed is not a self-serving ability. It is more about tending to and strengthening our relationships with others.

Think about a relationship you have today that feels so broken that any thoughts of repairing it seem as hard as replanting a full-grown redwood or relocating a mountain. The roots of your resentment run deep, digging into your soul and anchoring themselves to your spirit. The memories of that pain define your horizon, and they are the first thing you see when you peer into tomorrow.

When Jesus says all we need is a little bit of faith, like the size of a seed, to move that tree and mountain, we are right to scoff. The heartache is too harsh, the sadness too severe.

But think about what having a seed means. It means that inside its shell is the organic potential to bloom new possibilities. It means you hold in your hand the promise of new life. All you have to do is unleash it.

After that, it's up to God to do the work—to water that seed until the casing cracks and the first shoot pokes through the ground. To give it enough sunlight to trigger its growth. To nourish the ground so that tiny seed becomes the tree that provides shade and fruit for others to enjoy.

Forgiveness means doing your part and entrusting the rest to God. It means resisting the urge to lash back at those who have caused harm to you and to others, and choosing instead to let the power of God's grace work over time. The hope, of course, is that God will work in the other person's life as well because you can't change that person, no matter how hard you try. Only God can.

Over time, you'll discover that the impossible work of rebuilding a relationship is possible after all.

God, you know that my relationships with others can be difficult. I offer to you my commitment to forgive others, as well as to stop causing harm to others, trusting that you will give me strength. Amen.

What steps can you take today to release that mustard seed of faith and forgiveness and allow God to help rebuild your relationships?

DAY 22

Luke 17:11-19

THE KEY TO DEEPER HEALING

These ten people needed healing in an obvious way. They were suffering from leprosy, a very common but menacing disease that began with a bacterial infection of the skin that then moved to the nervous system. The bacteria would eventually spread to the extremities—the hands and feet—causing the most visible signs of infection: the twisting of the limbs, the curling of the fingers, the claw of the hand. The face would also be affected, with the thickening of the ear and the collapsing of the nose, followed by tumors on the skin and airways.

Worst of all, because the leprosy bacteria attacked the nervous system, a person would eventually lose the ability to see as the optic nerve would deteriorate, lose the ability to feel pain as the pain receptors would be shut down, and no longer be able to see or feel the steady deterioration of their own bodies.

Because it was transmitted through physical contact, lepers were often forced to live only among other lepers, so it is not surprising that these ten were together when they heard that Jesus was among them. It also makes sense that they kept their distance from Jesus, when they started calling out to him, "Jesus, Master, show us mercy!" (Luke 17:13).

What is interesting about the way Jesus healed the lepers is how surprisingly unoriginal his methods were. In other healing stories, Jesus had a flare for the dramatic, spitting on the ground and applying mud to a blind man, or drawing in the dirt to build suspense, or uttering in Aramaic before raising a little girl from the dead.

But here? Nothing special. He kept his distance, and all he did was tell them to turn around and walk away, going to show themselves to the priests who would pronounce them clean. As they walked away, every step that took them farther away from Jesus brought them closer and closer to healing.

Or did it?

Sometimes it's not the obvious illnesses that require the deepest healing but the ones that are often unseen, the ones that only God can diagnose. That's why Luke has more story to tell us. He would want us to remember that suffering with leprosy was not just physical, neurological, or superficial. It was emotional, social, and relational. In a real sense, their illness was spiritual.

Leprosy carried a severe social stigma. Ancient communities would sometimes affix a bell to the neck of a person with leprosy and force them to walk on certain sides of the street, depending on the direction of the wind blowing, for fear that the contagion would be spread by air. To be a leper was to live the life of an outcast, shunned by society as subhuman.

Because they had lost their ability to see, lepers could not see the looks of horror and rejection from everyone around them. Because they could not feel, they could not know the touch of another human being.

All of this meant that lepers felt less than human. Worthless. Rejected. Like God had made a mistake when God made them. Many of them must have felt like there was no purpose to life, like they were simply taking up space. Forget about the physical ailments related to leprosy. The deeper thing they needed healing from was spiritual, emotional, and deeply personal.

This story suggests that only one of the ten found that kind of healing.

Only one of them turned around. Only one decided to do something that previously was impossible. He returned to Jesus and got close to him. He bowed before Jesus' feet, and he said thank you.

It's here at this moment that Jesus chooses his words very carefully. He said, "Weren't ten cleansed? Where are the other nine?" (Luke 17:17). And then he said, "Get up and go. Your faith has healed you" (Luke 17:19).

Notice. Nine of them were cleansed. Only one was *healed*. Nine of them were able to receive wholeness and health for their obvious ailments. But only one received healing for the deeper ailment.

The other nine might have had perfectly good reasons for what they did. Maybe one of them went straight to his family to give them the great news. Maybe another one went to try to get a job for the first time. Maybe another went straight to the other lepers to give them the possibility of hope and promise. Their reasons might have been perfectly understandable, but only one of them experienced a deeper healing.

The one who came back to thank Jesus is the only one who felt his dignity restored, his sense of identity redeemed, and his connection to life and purpose and meaning repaired in a deep way. It could only happen when he was grateful to God.

Gratitude heals.

God, thank you. Thank you for the many obvious blessings in my life. Call to my mind those things that I often take for granted, that I might be even more grateful to you. Amen.

What are the deeper ways that you need healing in your emotions, your mind, and your spirit?

DAY 23
Luke 17:20-37
CLOSER THAN YOU THINK

When I was a teenager, in my church youth group, one of our favorite games to play was "Hide and Go Seek in the Dark." It was a variation of the popular children's game, except all the lights were turned off all around the church campus. Those who went into hiding tucked themselves into a corner of darkened rooms, under furniture and, in some cases, simply stood in the middle of the room with the lights off. The "seeker" then began the hunt, with the only stipulation that he or she was not permitted to turn any lights on.

You can imagine the hilarity. The seeker would often enter the room, tiptoeing to listen for the faintest movement or slightest breath. With the lights off, the seeker was often completely unaware that the people hiding were mere feet—or even inches—away.

At the end of each round, with every person found, the debrief was often filled with laughter.

"You had no idea how close you were to finding us!"

"We were right there the whole time!"

"You nearly stepped on my foot!"

In Luke 17, Jesus describes for the disciples a high-stakes game of Hide and Go Seek in the Dark. He is describing the arrival and presence of the kingdom of God in such a way as to suggest that even though it is already here and pervasive, it is also very difficult to see.

"God's kingdom isn't coming with signs that are easily noticed. Nor will people say, 'Look, here it is!' or 'There it is!' Don't you see? God's kingdom is already among you" (Luke 17:20-21).

The answer, of course, is no. No, the disciples don't see it. We don't see it. We aren't able to see it because it's too dark in the world. Maybe we are not looking in the right place. Or maybe we are too frustrated with the darkness. Or maybe we've just given up looking altogether. But Jesus says the kingdom of God is here, out of plain view.

Or does he? No sooner does he talk about the hiddenness of the kingdom than he pivots and talks about some signs that surely no one would miss. A flash of lighting in the sky. The appearance of the Son of God. Then he draws parallels with the Old Testament: a massive flood wiping out the earth. Fire from heaven destroying Sodom and Gomorrah. Two people in bed, then one person disappears. Two women in the field, then one of them vanishes.

I mean, really. Those seem like pretty obvious signs to me.

How do we reconcile these two ideas from Jesus? Is the kingdom of God hard to spot or not? Is the presence of God's power and love hidden, or is it obvious?

To discern the answer, consider the stories that are on either side of this passage. Beforehand is the story of the ten lepers, in which only one comes back grateful after he is healed. And what follows is the story of a widow who persistently pleads with a judge until he grants her justice.

What do those two stories have in common? Struggle. Suffering. It is only in going through leprosy that the one healed man could realize what a gift his health from Jesus really was. And it was only in engaging the struggle against unfairness and a stubborn judge that the woman was able to find justice.

In these words from today's Scripture reading, what do lightning, floods, and fire all have in common? They are examples of struggle and suffering.

Maybe what Jesus is saying here is not that the darkness is the thing that prevents us from seeing signs of God's presence and power. Maybe darkness is the gateway. Maybe this isn't a game of Hide and Go Seek in the Dark after all. Maybe there are times in our life when the spiritual life is more like a game of Find Only in the Dark.

If you are going through a particularly tough time of uncertainty in your life at the moment, Jesus' words are an invitation to embrace it, not hide from it. As you enter and embrace that darkness, do you know what you will discover? God is right there. Closer to you than you think.

God, thank you for meeting me in the darkness. I long to find your kingdom in and around me, even amid the struggles of my life. Amen.

In what ways do you feel like your life is filled with darkness today? What can you do to surrender yourself to God and allow Jesus to lead you through that darkness?

DAY 24

Luke 18:1-14

NO WIMPY PRAYERS

This is a woman who had the chips stacked against her. First, we know she was a widow. In her culture, that meant she had no voice. She was not able to stand up for herself when something happened to her. Then, someone wronged her. We don't know the details, but someone took whatever little dignity she had left as a down-and-out, discarded member of society and left her now with absolutely nothing.

But there is one thing this woman had that was not stolen from her. She still maintained a sense of dogged determination. No matter what was happening to her, no matter what the odds were, there was no way she was ever going to give up trying. She wanted justice. She wanted her wrongs to be righted.

So, she followed the only course of action available to her in that time, which was go to the institution of justice—the local judge—to plead her case.

We know very little about the judge this widow went to, but we know enough to know that this is someone we wouldn't like too much. This judge "neither feared God nor respected people" (Luke 18:2). Here was a person whose job it was to care for people who were wronged, to oversee the proper allocation of justice in the community, and this person did not fear God or care too much about people. And this poor widow had no one to turn to but this judge.

Now, the stage has been set. Or it's more like the wrestling ring has been set. In one corner, you have the big, bad, mean, corrupt, evil judge. Probably tall, probably muscular, probably scowling. In the other corner, you have the poor widow, who has already been hurt deeply by someone else. She has no money to bribe things her way and no husband to give her credibility in the community.

The bell rings, the combatants commence, and the woman pleads her case. "Give me justice in this case against my adversary," the woman says (Luke 18:3).

The woman kept coming to him. "Give me justice in this case against my adversary," she kept pleading. But the judge continued to say no.

For normal people, that would have ended it. This widow should have gone home defeated and dejected. But despite having no voice, despite having no money, she had one thing that kept her in the fight: determination and persistence.

So she met the judge at the courthouse. Hers was the first face he saw when stepped out the door: "Give me justice in this case against my adversary." I imagine she followed him down the street, calling out her request nonstop. She probably "bumped" into him at the fruit market, yelling in his ear as he was squeezing his figs. She knew where he lived. She dogged him in his own house. She knocked on his door, called out his name, tied messages to his pets, carved phrases in his matzah, and hid notes in his mailbox saying, "Give me justice in this case against my adversary." She did everything she possibly could to get her way.

Finally, the judge said to himself, "I don't fear God or respect people, but I will give this widow justice because she keeps bothering me. Otherwise, there will be no end to her coming here and embarrassing me" (Luke 18:4-5). The English language doesn't capture this fully. The Greek word translated here as "embarrassing me" can also mean "wear me out" (NRSV), and it's probably better translated in boxing terms. Its literal meaning involves giving someone a black eye or otherwise striking someone in the face. In other words, "I'll grant her justice because she's liable to beat the living tar out of me if I don't give her what she wants."

How about that? The weakling wins. She doesn't win because of strength but because of determination. Not because of might but because of persistence in asking.

Jesus says that is exactly how we should pray to God for justice.

You and I may be used to quieter, more somber prayers. We may be used to payers that are more like scribbling messages, stuffing them into corked bottles, and launching them into a skeptical ocean.

But the model of prayer most common in the Bible is none of these things. It is prayer that is shaped by the whirlwind of human emotional dynamics. Our prayers are most effective when they are most reflective of what we are truly feeling. Prayers should incorporate the realities of our anguish, our anger, our bitterness, our euphoria, and all the recklessly wild, stampeding emotions that course through our veins.

Jesus did not believe in wimpy prayers because Jesus did not believe that prayers were wimpy. Jesus believed that there was a power so strong in the act of prayer that it demands our fullest attention and the fullest participation of our emotional capabilities. The woman made her requests of the judge by pouring out every real emotion contained in her frightened body, and so should we.

God, teach me to pray with tenacity and courage. Help me not to lose heart, even when the situation gets tougher. Amen.

In what ways are you like the persistent widow? How would you like to be even more like her?

DAY 25

Matthew 19:13-15; Mark 10:13-16; Luke 18:15-17

THE UPSIDE-DOWN KINGDOM

This episode of Jesus and the children is one of those stories that is recorded in Matthew, Mark, and Luke. There are a few variations among them, but the core of the story is the same. Some people brought their children to Jesus so that he might bless them, but the disciples stepped in.

"Whoa, wait a minute, parents. What do you think this is? A daycare? A circus? Adults only, folks."

In Mark, that was enough to make Jesus *angry*. That's the word that Mark alone uses (Mark 10:14), as Matthew and Luke don't care to give us an insight into Jesus' frame of mind. But Mark is clear. The forbidding of children made Jesus downright upset.

Why?

Well, perhaps some background might help.

The Roman Empire was the preeminent, most powerful, and richest empire in the entire world at the time. But let me give you a quick snapshot of the kinds of conditions that Roman children were potentially subjected to.

If a child was born that the father of that family didn't want, then the father, who was the head of the household, had to make a choice. Sometimes children were born out of wedlock, or as the result of an affair, or from a surprise pregnancy. Sometimes the child was considered defective in some way, or perhaps wasn't the son that the father was hoping for to guarantee him an heir. The father could choose to give up the child.

In Roman times, giving up the child sometimes meant handing it off to become a slave. Other times it meant simply abandoning the child near garbage dumps to fend for itself or be picked up by just about anyone willing to take in that child. Sometimes it would be the most unscrupulous people who would pick up these kids, then force them into slavery, prostitution, or to be gladiators in the stadiums.

In other words, back in Roman times, children were easily construed as the bottom of the bottom. They were beneath even the slaves. They were simply property, with no rights of their own, no way of determining their future, no way of charting their own course.

With that background, we come to today's text. We think it's about parents bringing their children to Jesus so that he could bless them.

But the original Greek says nothing about these people being parents. It doesn't say these children belonged to these people. In fact, the word "bringing" could suggest that these people were bringing children to Jesus to seek healing because there was something wrong with them. In other words, it is possible that Jesus was saying these words near a refuse site, where a crowd had gathered, including some of these children, who were the lowest of the low.

And what is it that Jesus said?

"Allow the children to come to me. Don't forbid them, because God's kingdom belongs to people like these children" (Mark 10:14).

No, this is not a Norman Rockwell painting. This is not Mother Goose gathering children together for story time.

This is a scathing editorial. This is Michael Moore meets Quentin Tarantino. This is shock theater with a purpose. It is not meant to solicit oohs and aahs, but gasps and gulps.

What does this guy think he's doing? It's one thing to associate with these children, these lower-than-low pieces of property. But Jesus went one step further: He said that to these children the kingdom of God belongs. The great riches of God, the mighty love and amazing grace of God, belong not to the rich, the powerful, the esteemed, the famous, or the ones on the top. Jesus took the entire hierarchy of the Roman cultural establishment and flipped it upside down. The kingdom of God belongs to these children, the ones on the bottom.

That's why, of all the controversial things that Jesus ever said, this was one of the most scandalous.

Rather than rejecting these children, sending them out of the household, and sentencing them to a life of misery, suffering, and possible death, Jesus welcomed them with open arms and said, "You are my children. You are part of my household. You are part of my kingdom."

You want a definition of the kingdom of God? How about this: the kingdom of God is that reality that claims every child as part of God's family. For every child deserves a chance to experience compassion, unconditional love, and a future with hope.

Every child, in the words of the Gospel, can be blessed.

God, thank you for welcoming the children. Enable me to work for justice, love, and compassion for all children, all around the world. Teach me to have faith like a child. Amen.

How have you witnessed children relegated to the bottom of the power structure in your community?

DAY 26

Matthew 19:16-22; Mark 10:17-22; Luke 18:18-23

MORE THAN RICHES

Whoever this man was, he certainly made an impression on three of the Gospel writers. He is popularly known as "the rich man," mostly because Matthew, Mark, and Luke all agree about his wealth but don't bother revealing to us his name. Maybe it's because, in his anonymity, there is universality. We may not be as rich as he was, but we can each identify with his spiritual condition. His name might as well be ours.

He approached Jesus with a fairly straightforward question, about how to secure eternal life. He was not only wanting to ask, "How can I live beyond death?" but also, "How can I really live life?" That's the central question for most of us. If we're not worried about what will happen after we die, we are regularly fixated on how to maximize our time when we are alive.

Jesus knows it. His answer to the man does not center so much on postmortem eternity as it addresses living the "complete" life (Matthew 19:21) and the one thing the man lacks (Mark 10:21).

But Jesus' answer also packs a surprising punch: living the perfect life, whole and complete and free of need, has nothing to do with your money. In fact, Jesus tells the man, money actually may be standing in your way, and what you may have to do is free yourself from it. That's why, upon hearing this answer, the man walked away sorrowful.

Years ago, I took my two daughters to the Philippines to visit our ancestral homeland. As one born in the United States, I had visited the Philippines nearly forty years ago as a child, and I was eager to meet many relatives I had not remembered.

One of the highlights was a visit to my mother's childhood neighborhood, a two-and-a-half-hour car ride from our hotel, followed by a two-hour boat ride to my mother's home island of Mindoro.

Her home is still standing there, now occupied by extended family members. It is a very modest home in a barrio called Silonay, a small village with about 250 families.

The barrio was accessible only by a half-mile-long footbridge, which we crossed with the services of a rented bicyclist who allowed us to ride in his sidecar. Everything people need in the barrio, from their food, to their furnishings, to their lumber for construction, gets hauled over that little bridge into a village of houses.

The houses were clustered together, with no organized layout or perpendicular streets. Instead, the houses were all arranged around common areas, water pumps, courtyards, clothes washing stations. Everyone knew everyone.

And do you want to know something?

Everywhere I looked, people were smiling.

We walked into my mother's home, currently occupied by her first cousin Boy Rojas, my uncle. The house was spartan but clean. No cable television, no air conditioning, no extravagance. There was a very small refrigerator, and there was a stovetop to do the cooking. He took me into the bedroom, and I saw a very well kept, tidy room with simple furniture.

You might think in a situation like this there would be lots of reason for misery. The people there know how people in other parts of the world live, with their cars, big houses, and the means to travel and purchase without care. But I want you to know, Boy Rojas had a bigger smile on his face than just about anyone I've ever met.

Here's why.

He took me into one room where he had displayed three pictures. They were pictures of his three daughters, each of them in her college graduation gown. He beamed with pride, telling me about one daughter who graduated with an MBA and is now working in finance. He told me about another daughter with a degree in health care, and another one who works in accounting. He said to me, "I don't have a lot of money. I'm pretty poor. But look at my daughters. They are doing well now." And he beamed.

I was overcome with amazement by my uncle. I wanted to quibble with him. ("But you are rich, uncle. Rich in spirit, and in family, and in joy.") But the last thing he needed to hear was a person like me, family member or otherwise, trying to convince him how rich he really was. He would know that I was really just trying to convince myself.

Instead, we just looked at each other for a few seconds. He nodded his head, and he smiled.

Deep down inside, I was jealous, longing for that kind of contentment apart from wealth and possessions.

I'm not rich, I'm not young, and I'm far from being a ruler of any kind. But maybe the reason Matthew, Mark, and Luke all tell this man's story is that many of us can identify with his reaction.

After viewing his own earthly riches, in relation to the riches of the kingdom, he "was dismayed at this statement and went away saddened, because he had many possessions" (Mark 10:22).

God, thank you for creating me to live with joy and contentment. Empower me to live more simply, that I might experience true life in your Spirit. Help me to prioritize people over possessions, and relationships over riches. Amen.

What people have you known whose contentment and happiness was centered on something other than wealth and possessions? How is God calling you to simplify your life of excess?

Matthew 20:1-16

THE ECONOMICS OF GRACE

On schoolyard blacktops all across the country, during a typical lunch-hour recess, a familiar scene unfolds. Boys and girls, ready for a quick game of basketball, pause in their warm-up shoot-around for that all-too-familiar, all-too-painful pre-game ritual: the picking of the teams.

The captains step up, taking turns picking players for their team from the draft pool they have before them. One by one, the remaining kids go from a wistful, hopeful "Pick me! Pick me!" to a jubilant, fist-pumping "Yes!" as they go to join their new team.

Then, in the end, there are the final few.

They strain to hold back a pained look in their eyes, but it's no surprise. They knew they would be here. They knew they would be among the last, but the sting still hurts. They know they aren't the most talented, the most gifted, the most skilled ball players, but they can contribute if they could only have a chance. Eventually, all the kids are picked, some because of their skills and others because they had to be.

That's the way life is, isn't it? There's a pecking order to things. The best folks, the prettiest, the most popular, the strongest, the fastest, the wisest, the flashiest, they get picked first.

But imagine a reversal.

What would you think if, at the end of every fiscal quarter, an employer awarded the highest bonuses to those who sold the fewest products? Or what if a sports team began to give more playing time to the rookie players who just arrived, rather than the lifetime veterans who have proven themselves on the field? What if schools started granting honor roll awards to students regardless of their grades, saying, "As long as you got anything between an A and a D-, you'll get a certificate"?

Would you think it ludicrous? Would you think it unfair? Would you cry foul?

Imagine how the disciples must have felt. Jesus told a story about how unfair the grace of God really is. He told them a story of a landowner who sat down with some laborers and negotiated a contract with them.

He said essentially, "OK, here's a vineyard. You work here starting at 6 a.m. and I'll pay you this much for the day." They got to work, and then another shift of workers arrived at 9 a.m. A third shift arrived at noon. Soon, 6 a.m. workers were working side by side with the 9 a.m. workers and the noon arrivals. Then at 5 p.m., another group of workers arrived, and they helped finish out the rest of the day.

At evening time, the landowner settled the pay with the workers, and this is where the ludicrousness occurred. The landowner paid the *same salary* to everyone. Those who had worked all day got the same as those who had worked half a day, and the same as those who had worked only a few hours.

The early arrivers grumbled. "This isn't fair; we should've been paid more. We worked harder; we made a greater contribution. We proved ourselves out on the field. We were picked first."

But the landowner sealed the discussion with a truth that they could not deny. The landowner paid everyone everything that they were promised. Not a penny more and not a penny less. The employer determined the pay, and he delivered. These days an employer like that would probably be sued for violating some fair labor law.

Yet there is no denying Matthew's fundamental point. The economy of the world is not the economy of grace. The world would say that we needed to reward the fittest and discard the lowliest. We would revere those that are most gifted, who had been at it the longest, who have made the greatest contributions. We would forget about the ones at the bottom.

Grace knows no strict hierarchies. It acknowledges each life as one in need of God's love. Whether you are a longtime Christian, who has been in the church since the morning hours of your youth, or whether you are a new arrival, blooming to full faith in the evening hours of your life, you are regarded the same by a loving God who gives the contract. This God owns the field. This God made the fields.

The economy of grace suggests that the first will be last and the last will be first. It suggests that we are never to disregard someone who doesn't seem well seasoned in the faith, whose life is too marred by sin, or who doesn't seem to measure up to some churchy standard.

In God's eyes, everyone is acceptable because everyone is accepted by God.

God, thank you for your grace, which loves me regardless of my past. Remind me to treat others with love, just as you love me. Amen.

How do you identify with the late-arriving workers? How do you identify with the early-arriving workers?

DAY 28

Matthew 20:20-28; Mark 10:35-45

SPELLING SERVANTHOOD

If only the Gospel writers had videographers. Then we might have gotten a glimpse of the faces of the other disciples as James, John, and their mother were making their request of Jesus. We imagine the furrowed eyebrows and laser-beam glares of the other ten as the Zebedees asked if they could assume a place of prominence in what they figured was Jesus' imminent regime. The others must have shaken their heads and rolled their eyes, even murmured under their breath.

"Who do those boys think they are?"

Jesus, of course, would have nothing of it. In fact, he used their request as an opportunity to teach them—and all of us—a lesson. That lesson would be at the core of Jesus' identity and mission on earth.

He did not come to be served, but to serve—to give his life for others.

It's interesting that when I type the word *servanthood* in my word processing program, a red squiggly line appears underneath it. It's an indication that I must have misspelled a word or written a non-English word. I have come to realize that my program doesn't recognize the word *servanthood*. It is a visual reminder of just how foreign a word it is to my computer, just as it is a foreign concept to our culture.

We don't understand why someone would want to seek the benefit of others and the community around him, rather than his own interests. We don't see why someone would want to use her skills and abilities for the sake of others regardless of payment or compensation. We don't see why someone would choose not to be served but to serve, lose her life in order to gain it, or choose to be last instead of first.

Servanthood is not the same as service. It's more than just what we do with our hands and the nice things we do for other people.

Servanthood is much deeper than that. It cuts to our motivations, our priorities, and the way we perceive other people, including our family and friends, the strangers in our midst, and the world around us.

What Jesus said must have been shocking to the disciples, just as it should be a shock to us. In Jesus' day, just as in our day, there was a clearly understood pecking order. At the top were those who were served: Caesar, the governors, the senators, the generals. Basically, the bosses. At the bottom? Basically, everyone else

But in that one dramatic statement, Jesus flipped that entire paradigm upside down. If you want to be first, you've got to be last. If you want to be great, you've got to be a servant. If you want true life, you must lose your life for the sake of others. The only way to do that is through a mind of servanthood, in which you put aside your own selfish agendas for the sake of the common good.

It means, first of all, emptying yourself.

Consider for a moment what things you need to be emptied of in order to be filled with the power, purpose, and plan of God to be revealed in your life. It could be resentment about something that's been bothering you about your past, your family, or even your job. It could be anger, regret, anxiety, or grief. To live as a servant for other people, which is the highest calling of a follower of Jesus, we have to lay aside everything that would suggest "it's all about me."

But it's not just self-emptying. It's also self-acceptance.

There may be aspects of your life right now that you are ashamed of, which you feel make you too weak, too powerless, too ill-equipped, to possibly make a difference in the world out there. Maybe you feel like your position is not important enough, your influence is not great enough, or your weakness is not surmountable enough for you to be of any good.

Servanthood not only means laying aside your selfishness; it also means surrendering your weakness. When you can accomplish both of those things, then imagine all that God can do through you.

You have been given a unique set of skills, a unique set of abilities, to serve others and offer yourself for the benefit of those in need.

Whether you know it or not, you can be a servant, following the example of Jesus.

God, thank you for sending us the example of Christ, who gave himself for us. Help me to live as one who serves in all I do, with everyone I know. Amen.

What difference do you think it would make if more people in the world assumed a servant's mindset?

DAY 29

Matthew 20:29-34; Mark 10:46-50; Luke 18:35-43

AN ENCOUNTER BETWEEN ROYALTY

This is not the only miracle story involving the healing of a blind person, but it may be the most intriguing. Mark is the only one to give us his name, an aspect of his life that he feels so important that he emphasizes it twice. The man's name is Bartimaeus, Mark tells us. Then Mark tells us that he is the son of Timaeus. Never mind the fact that Bartimaeus itself means "Son of Timaeus." Mark wants to make doubly sure that we get that point.

Why? Well, it might have something to do with the fact that *Timaeus* is derived from the Greek word for *honorable*. Mark may be inviting us to conclude that this woeful blind man has an honorable ancestry, a distinguished lineage that really should have set him up for a life of prestige and comfort. Instead, the tragic irony is that his physical condition has betrayed his name. His blindness has brought him dishonor, since blind people were often pushed to the fringes of society, marginalized outside of people's compassion and concern.

That's why Luke's and Matthew's versions of the story specifically state that Jesus and the disciples met Bartimaeus *outside* Jericho, as they were drawing near to the city. He was a man who was pushed to the outskirts of the town, so as not to be visible to its citizens. His physical condition had brought him shame and embarrassment, made even more tragic by his very name.

This is a man who should have been royalty. Instead, he was rejected.

Maybe it takes a person with a royal title to know another person with a royal title. Because as soon as the blind son of an honorable man found out that Jesus was within earshot, he called out with a loud voice:

"Jesus, Son of David..." (Mark 10:47).

The Gospel writers are creating an encounter between two parallel lives. The first is the son of an honorable man who was rejected for his condition. The second is the Son of an Honorable Ancestor. The Son of David. The Son of God, in fact, who would be rejected by taking on the condition of the world.

It is no surprise, then, that Mark and Matthew tell this story right before Jesus enters Jerusalem to begin his final week on earth. This encounter with Bartimaeus is much more than just another healing miracle of just another man. There were other blind people Jesus healed in the Gospels, after all. That is not what makes this story unusual. What sets this one apart is that in Bartimaeus, Jesus may have seen a little bit of himself. In this blind man is someone torn between prestige and pain, between status and suffering, between royalty and rejection.

Do you know what? I think that may be the same way that Jesus looks at you.

Your name may not be Bartimaeus, but you certainly are a child of royalty. Within you is God's very own image, the imprint of the divine right within the essence of your being. It doesn't mean that you are God or that you are equal with God. But it means that you have within you the capacity to reflect the royalty of God in your actions and your attitudes.

But all of us are blind. We are blind to the presence of God within us. We are blinded by the presence of violence and selfishness that saturate our world. We are blinded by the wrong things we do and by the right things that we fail to do.

We are blinded by our sin.

I also find it fascinating that in Matthew's version of the story, we are told there are *two* blind people. Their blindness was shared in community, in relationship. That just might accurately describe your condition too. You may be in a relationship that is broken by bitterness, hurt, and despair. You may be living in a community that is blinded by racism, prejudice, and injustice. It's one thing to be blind by yourself. It's quite another to be blind and to have no one around you who is able to see.

The most interesting part of this miracle story, of course, is this statement: "What do you want me to do for you?" (Mark 10:51).

Jesus requires the man (or men) to name their need, even though it really ought to be obvious. In fact, it would have been downright tragic, if not utterly comical, if Bartimaeus had said, "You know, Jesus, I'm really fine, but I've got a bit of a cold." Or, "If it's no trouble, I've got a mosquito bite that's annoying me."

Why do you suppose Jesus asked him a question with an utterly obvious answer? I don't think it's because Jesus needed to know the answer. I think it's because he needed to know the way Bartimaeus would answer it.

In all three Gospels, the man (or men) clearly states his need, which he was powerless to achieve on his own. Bartimaeus was the passive recipient, and he knew Jesus was the active doer. Bartimaeus acknowledged that he had no right to demand healing, and no reason to think he could do anything to make himself well. The only thing he had to do was surrender, to be the recipient. His eyes needed to be opened, and only Jesus could do that.

Apparently, that was the right answer, because it was exactly what Jesus was wanting to hear.

So, what do you need Jesus to do, in you and through you?

God, thank you for creating me as your child. But I feel blind, unable to see your presence in my life and the hope that you have for me. Help me to name my condition through confession and obedience. Teach me to trust in you. Amen.

What difference does it make for you to remember that you are a child of God, offspring of honor?

DAY 30

Matthew 25:14-30; Mark 13:33-37; Luke 19:11-28

DON'T BURY YOUR CALLING

Jesus tells a story of a master who did an unusual thing one day. He was a very wealthy man, and he decided to go on a trip. He needed to figure out what to do with his treasure.

What would you do if you were that man? You couldn't put your money in the bank. Banks in those days weren't like the banks we have now. They weren't safe and secure, and there was no guarantee you'd get your money back. Take your money with you on the trip? Well, fat chance.

Some translations record this amount of money as a "talent," one of the highest amounts of currency in the entire ancient Near Eastern culture. A single talent was the same value as the sum of over sixteen years' worth of income. We are talking about a lot of money.

Of course, there were no bills, no paper currency back then. Instead, goods and currency were exchanged with coins, and a talent would have been many coins, and very heavy. There was no way this guy was taking his money with him.

The only other alternative would have been for him to leave his money with someone he could trust—a family member or a rich friend. But he chose not to. This master—and this God whom the master represents—does the absolute shocking thing. He does something that is absolutely countercultural to the time. He entrusts this entire fortune to his servants.

Here is the first surprising thing we learn about God: God is exceedingly generous to a people who don't deserve it. God has elevated us servants to the status of family, as children of God, by entrusting to us the care of God's greatest fortune: the kingdom of God. "No longer do I call you servants," Jesus said, "for a servant does not know what his master is doing; but I have called you friends" (John 15:15 NKJV)

Here's another way to think about it. This parable suggests that God needs you.

Well, you know what happens next. The first servant is given five talents, the equivalent of $2.5 million, and he turns around and invests it. He doubles it to ten talents, $5 million. The second servant is given $1 million, and he turns it into $2 million.

Here is the second surprising thing we learn about God: the master was uncharacteristically effusive in his praise of the first two servants when they brought back a return on his money. A master simply did not say such glowing words to a slave in public as the ones that the master uttered: "Excellent! You are a good and faithful servant!" (Matthew 25:21).

But the third servant doesn't get it. Do you want to know what the biggest problem with the third servant is? It's not that he buried the money. I mean, that was relatively commonplace back then. Without a trusted bank, without rich family or friends, that's what you did in those days to protect your money. You buried it. Nothing wrong with that. Jesus told another story about a man who had a pearl of great value. What did he do with it? He buried it in a field. Nothing wrong with that.

Do you want to know what the third servant's biggest problem was? He didn't believe that his master really needed him.

"I knew that you are a hard man," he said, which is another way of saying, "I knew you were able to do whatever you wanted. You could make anything happen. You can harvest where you didn't sow. You could reap where you didn't scatter seed. Who am I to make a contribution to someone who could do anything?"

If you and I are honest today, that's what our problem is too. How could God possibly need me? you might ask. What would God possibly want or expect from someone like me? God can do anything. God can harvest without sowing, reap without scattering seed. Now God is entrusting to you and to me the riches of the kingdom, expecting us to build it, shape it, advance it? You've got to be kidding!

No wonder the third servant said, "So I was afraid."

This is a story for each of us, for we have been entrusted to build the Kingdom. All the while, the forces of evil, sin, and suffering are swirling all around us, and we find ourselves saying to the Master, "You're expecting us to do this? You've got to be kidding."

Nope. God is not kidding at all. Our part in the Kingdom is no laughing matter.

God, thank you for calling me to such a high and holy purpose in your kingdom. Help me to overcome my ambivalence and to trust you in all I do. Amen.

What do you think about the notion that God is entrusting you with such an important responsibility to help build the Kingdom?

DAY 31

John 12:1-8

TEAM MARY OR TEAM JUDAS?

At the heart of this story is an argument between a man and a woman who see the same situation in completely different terms. It's not a disagreement based on gender lines, even though they happen to be different sexes. It's not about a petty issue because we get the sense from John that what they are arguing about is critical to understanding the meaning and message of Jesus, along with the importance of Holy Week just around the corner.

Jesus arrives in a home, he gets anointed with oil, and then there is a disagreement about the significance of the act. And whereas the other Gospels render the characters in the story anonymous, John wants to name names. The woman with the perfume is Mary of Bethany, the sister of Martha and Lazarus. Not Mary Magdalene and not Mary the mother of Jesus. This is the Mary with wanderlust, her head in the clouds—dreaming, worshiping, imaginative Mary. She emptied an expensive jar of perfume on Jesus.

As soon as she performs this act, she is immediately rebuked by Judas Iscariot, and suddenly we would recognize what these two names represent. John is constructing a marquee matchup between two high-profile, star-studded people who happen to be among Jesus' closest friends. We might imagine it as a sort of Madison Square Garden–style billing. This is LeBron James vs. Kobe Bryant. Martina Navratilova vs. Chris Evert Lloyd. Manny Pacquiao vs. Floyd Mayweather. Or Bugs Bunny vs. Elmer Fudd.

You get the picture. By naming names, John escalates the scene into an attention-grabbing, headline-seizing match-up at the very beginning.

He wants us to choose sides. Are you Team Mary or Team Judas? If you're on team Mary, that means you get it. You understand something that the rest of the world doesn't quite seem to get: the essence of Jesus' mission, the purpose for his coming to earth.

If you look at a variety of English translations of John 12:7, you'll discover a wide range of possible motivations for Mary's lavish perfume-act. Some translations have Jesus telling Mary, "Let her alone, so that she may keep it for the day of My burial" (NASB). In this version, Mary has no idea why she's dumping perfume on Jesus, and he has to tell her to save some of it because it might be handy later after he's dead.

Another translation has Jesus saying, "It was intended that she should save this perfume for the day of my burial" (NIV). Again, Jesus had to explain to Mary and to others what this perfume is really for.

In the Common English Bible translation, Jesus says, "Leave her alone. This perfume was to be used in preparation for my burial, and this is how she has used it." In other words, Mary knows *exactly* what she's doing. She gets it. She knows about Jesus' crucifixion and death, and his purpose for coming here. She knows that following him will ultimately lead to a cross.

Those on Team Judas don't get it. They refuse to acknowledge that the cross is a reality. They would prefer a sanitized, safer, and frankly more comfortable view of Jesus. He is the one who comforts and heals, the one who gives blessings and meets our needs. They like the talisman Jesus, who can be used for good luck. That was Judas's problem. He was hung up on the cost of the perfume and how the proceeds of its sale could help a few people. But he failed to see the cost of the cross and how Jesus' sacrificial, self-giving love could ultimately save the world.

At the heart of this story, then, is an invitation for you to choose: the way of Judas or the way of Mary. The Judas way, according to John, is the easier way. It denies the cost and risk associated with following Jesus. It seeks the abundant life without the life of discipleship, the life of blessing without a life of commitment.

The life Mary chose is the one that believes that if you want to gain your life, you must lose it. To truly live, you must die in Christ.

Nothing else in the world matters if you don't live a cross-shaped life. Being on Team Mary means you need to stop making everything about you and start living out God's purposes, God's best intentions for your life. It means putting to death your desire for greatness, power, and possession. It means putting to death your need to wipe out your enemies, and instead seeking reconciliation and forgiveness.

As musician Alison Krauss has sung, "Everybody wants to go to heaven, but nobody wants to die."

What parts of you need to die today?

God, thank you for the gift of Jesus, who surrendered his life in obedience to you. Help me to give my full commitment to you in all that I do. Amen.

In what ways are you like Mary in this story? How are you like Judas?

DAY 32

Matthew 21:1-11; Mark 11:1-11; Luke 19:29-44; John 12:12-19

PALM SUNDAY: SHRIEKING STONES

Jesus' entry into Jerusalem on the first Palm Sunday is of such significance that all four Gospel writers include it in their stories of Holy Week. It establishes the setting for the culmination of Jesus' earthly ministry, toward which Jesus set his face at the start of our Lenten journey.

It is a day we celebrate in our churches, but *celebrate* seems like an odd word. There is pageantry, praise, and rejoicing as we reimagine the joyous shouts of the people who lined the fabric-strewn streets with palms in their hands. But it is a celebration that would eventually turn sour, as the shouts of "Hosanna" would turn into "Crucify him" within a few days' time.

Maybe that is why Luke's rendition is so different from the other four. His is the only one that does not say a word about palm branches to begin with. Rather than focusing on the greenery in people's hands, he emphasizes the volume in their voices, saying that they praised God with a loud voice (Luke 19:37).

That aspect of the story is apparently so compelling to Luke that he alone records an interesting conversation between Jesus and the Pharisees during the processional. The Pharisees stand there, perceiving the people as lunatics running the asylum, and they've had enough. This, they believe, is a place for decorum and respect, not outward exuberance.

"Teacher, scold your disciples!" they told Jesus (Luke 19:39). Do something about these people who are clearly crossing the line. Tell them to behave.

That is what the world is often trying to tell the Church to do. Pipe down. Quit acting out. Fit into the prescribed mold. Quit advocating for peace; quit promoting the cause of the poor. Quit talking about nonviolence; quit professing your faith in Jesus. Quit trying to extend the hospitality of God to people on the fringe. Quit expressing your faith with such zeal and joy, when religion is supposed to be kept private. Do any of these statements sound familiar?

Well, Jesus has an interesting answer. If Jesus tried to silence the disciples, then the stones would resume the shouting.

I for one would have loved to have seen this. If I were a disciple, there's a part of me that would have wanted to clamp my mouth shut for a second and encourage others to do the same, just so I could see a rock come to life and start shouting. It would be the coolest, scariest thing ever.

But it wouldn't have been the first time a stone has shrieked. God has a hefty résumé of bringing life out of inanimate objects. God breathed life into a lump of clay to create human beings. God spoke judgment to Habakkuk through stone-filled walls. And in this Gospel, John the Baptist affirmed God's ability to raise Abraham's descendants from the stones (Luke 3:8).

Clearly, if the disciples went silent, the stones would be ready. You see, that's what happens in the kingdom of God. When one group of followers is silenced, there are others ready to take on the charge. When the world silences one witness, the cause is taken up by another at the ready.

Fortunately for Jesus, the disciples were not silent. They threw caution to the wind, displaying a free, unfettered enthusiasm, unencumbered by societal restriction or personal inhibition.

Something else that is interesting about Luke's Gospel is that he chose to place this Palm Sunday story right after the parable of the talents. Matthew puts Palm Sunday long before the parable. You remember the parable: a man gives out talents (money) to three individuals. The first two take their talents, take a risk, and come back with dividends. But the third man buries his talent, refuses to take a risk, chooses to stay comfortable, and comes back with nothing in return. He is sternly rebuked for it. Luke would want us to know that for any of us who enter this Holy Week, we need to behave with the same kind of commitment. We must be ready to take a risk, unafraid of cultural pressure and determined to live self-sacrificially rather than cautiously.

That is the message of Palm Sunday. It's not about the pageantry and pomp of palm fronds and adoring fans. The message is one of risk and self-sacrifice, which ultimately will lead us to a cross. Will you, who adore Jesus, take up the banner of love for the poor and the oppressed, the forsaken and the dying, the lost and the least? Will you be willing to lose your life—your priorities, your agendas, and even your most precious possessions—for the sake of advancing the good news to others?

If you don't, then we'll have to leave it up to the stones to do the work.

God, thank you for sending Jesus to die for us and to bring me into a closer relationship with you. Help me to live out my faith with boldness so that others might experience your love. Amen.

As you enter this Holy Week, what risk is God calling you to take for the benefit of others?

Matthew 21:12-14; Mark 11:11; Luke 19:45-48

COMMITTING WORSHIP THEFT

I will admit that this story tends to stump me. First, it is a bit disorienting to see such anger pour out of Jesus, since it's not an emotion we are accustomed to seeing from him in the Gospels. Then there is the whole business about what he was angry *about*. We aren't told explicitly in any of the Gospels why Jesus was so upset. All we really know is that Jesus saw something in the marketplace in the temple that made him angry enough to quote Isaiah and kick people out. We assume that means he was really angry.

It could have been that he was upset by the fact that there was commerce in the temple to begin with. Maybe the purist part of Jesus really wanted this ground to be kept as sacred as possible, apart from the economics of the secular world. But I'm not sure that's what this is about. People needed to make sacrifices. They needed animals to offer those sacrifices. This means they needed to purchase or trade for them if they didn't have them. And what better, more convenient place to buy your pigeons than right there, on site?

As the pastor of a local church, I can attest to the fact that on many Sundays, there is at least one enterprise or another where money changes hands. Easter lilies. Christmas poinsettias. Youth group Christmas trees. Vacation Bible School registrations. I would be hard pressed to imagine a campus completely free of booths, tables, displays, and money boxes. If that is the kind of thing that made Jesus really upset, then I think many churches had better bolt down their courtyard tables because Jesus apparently wants to flip them over.

Maybe Jesus was upset over the unethical business practices of the vendors. Maybe they were cheating people out of their money, overcharging for the livestock, price gouging according to the need.

That would certainly bring out the advocate in Jesus and upset him enough to overthrow the whole broken system. After all, he is upset enough to call them a bunch of robbers and thieves, so maybe they were stealing the people's precious financial resources for their own gain.

But if there is anything we have come to know about the Gospels, especially during this season of Lent, it is that the meaning of the story is much deeper than just the mere superficial.

What if Jesus was really upset about the way that people had lost their focus on the sacredness and spiritual purpose of worship? Maybe what had been "stolen" was the purity of worship itself, in exchange for purposes that were more self-serving.

I often hear of people who come to worship to get their spiritual pick-me-up for the week or to get their faith refueled after a tough week. There's nothing inherently wrong with that. I also hear about people who worship in order to learn how to be better people, better Christians, better parents, better coworkers, better friends. There's nothing inherently wrong with that, either.

But the more worship becomes about meeting *our needs*, making *ourselves* better people, and improving *our* lives, the less it becomes about the worship and praise of God and drawing us into an experience of God beyond ourselves. When we make worship more about us and less about God, we rob worship of its intended purpose.

What would it take to make worship a "house of prayer" again?

Think about Isaiah, whom the Gospel writers cite, whose call by God to be a prophet itself happened in the context of a worship experience. When he realized he was in the presence of God, his only response was to realize how unworthy he was: "Mourn for me; I'm ruined!" Isaiah proclaimed. "I'm a man with unclean lips, and I live among a people with unclean lips. Yet I've seen the king, the LORD of heavenly forces!" (Isaiah 6:5).

That's what it means to make one's life a "house of prayer." It means supplanting the self as the center of one's existence and acknowledging God as the center instead. When we place anything else in the way, as a barrier to giving wholehearted praise to God, then watch out. God will do whatever it takes to overturn those barriers. Worshiping anything other than God is nothing short of thievery.

God, thank you for creating me to worship you. Forgive me for placing other things and other people in the way. Help me overturn the tables in my heart, so that I might clear the room for me to praise you with my whole being. Amen.

What do you tend to make the object of your worship instead of God?

DAY 34

Matthew 21:18-27

THE FRUITLESS FIG TREE

Oh, that poor fig tree. Maybe it couldn't help it. Maybe it was diseased. Maybe it was planted in poor soil to begin with. Maybe whoever was supposed to tend to it didn't have a clue what to do. I know that if I were the gardener assigned to that fig tree, given my horrible history with plants, it would be doomed from the start.

Mark at least offers an explanation. When Jesus arrived at the tree, it wasn't the season for figs (Mark 11:13). The tree was green and leafy, but it wasn't bearing fruit because it wasn't the right time of year. Honestly, that makes Jesus' angry reaction that much more perplexing. How could anyone be justifiably upset when the tree was simply following the natural rhythms and seasons of its life?

Matthew doesn't seem interested at all in explaining why the tree wasn't bearing fruit because for him, the central part of this story is not the tree at all; it is the discussion about the tree that follows. Whereas Mark simply says that the disciples overheard Jesus talking to the tree, Matthew takes their interest one step further.

"How did the fig tree dry up so fast?" they ask (Matthew 21:20). Jesus, how in the world did you do that to the tree? They were much less interested in Jesus' anger, or the incapacity of the fig tree, and much more interested in how Jesus was able to order such dramatic change with just a spoken word.

Jesus told them they could do it "if you have faith and don't doubt." In fact, he says, with faith you can pick up a mountain and throw it in the sea, and whatever you ask for in prayer you will receive by faith (Matthew 21:21-22).

It suddenly becomes clear to us how Matthew intended to use this fig tree story. He wanted to teach us how to identify the rotten, decaying, unfruitful parts of our lives and the world, and how to prune them away, excising them from the world. All it takes is faith.

A few years ago, I met a man named Rick. As I got to know him, I learned a great deal about his life story. As the youngest child in his family, Rick was a boy with charm to equal his intelligence, a do-gooder and a hard worker, a people-oriented person.

Then, the realities of life swept in like a thief in the night. A tragic car accident forever altered his life, damaging his body and some of his capabilities. His father died suddenly just months after that accident. It was a burden of consecutive events far beyond what a normal teenager should have to bear. The fallout of these tragedies led to the darkest and most difficult period of his life, in which he battled with alcohol addiction.

His life soon became like that fig tree: unfruitful, with little chance of meeting his God-given potential.

But then, several years later, Rick experienced the powerful, transformative grace of God. It was then that Rick made the brave and bold decision to start a journey of recovery through the Alcoholics Anonymous twelve-step program.

What a journey that was. Slowly, Rick began to recover the brightness and bravery that marked his childhood. He was again able to become the affable, people-oriented, energetic guy as he became an inspiration to others who were themselves dealing with addiction. He remained sober and availed himself to speak to individuals and groups to be an encouragement for others. All the while, he became more and more passionate about his Christian conviction and wanted nothing more than to be fed in his faith and grow closer to Jesus.

When I first met him, he was bubbling to find his place of ministry in the church. "Well, Rick," I told him, "this isn't a flashy job, but it's an important one. We need help on Sundays helping people find a place to park. We need a friendly and helpful smile to greet people when they get out of their cars and welcome them to worship."

With every word, his eyes got brighter and his smile got bigger. "That's what I'll do!" he said. "Just let me know when to start." He added his passion and optimism to our hospitality ministry from then on.

Rick was diagnosed with cancer about a year later. With every treatment and every hospital visit, he continued to demonstrate that unwavering faith and indomitable sense of optimism and joy that would have been unlikely decades prior. But he was a changed man. All because of his faith in Jesus.

When I did his funeral service, it was an amazing celebration of his life. A huge number of people showed up to pay their tribute and give thanks for this man who was not only able to move mountains in his life, but also helped others do the same.

That's what Matthew is really interested in. Not the reasons why the fig tree didn't bloom. All of us have those problems in our lives. There's nothing unusual about that. It's what we choose to do about them that matters. By the power and grace of God, we can overcome them.

God, thank you for granting me the power to address the decaying and harmful parts of my life. Help me to have faith in you, that I can move the insurmountable mountains in my life and cast them into the sea. Amen.

What fig trees are you facing in your life today? What is God calling you to do to remove those unfruitful parts of your life and begin to bear fruit?

DAY 35

Matthew 21:28–22:14

STORIES OF TOUGH LOVE

Whew. Jesus has just about had it with the Pharisees. At least that's what Matthew would have us believe. Only in this Gospel do we hear Jesus respond to the Pharisees' incessant attempt to overthrow him. With three successive parables, Jesus throws down one gauntlet after another, a kind of rapid-fire, free-wheeling, no-holds-barred onslaught against the hypocrisy and harm he has seen from the religious leaders.

The first shot across the bow comes in the form of the parable of the two sons (Matthew 21:28-32). The father commanded them to get to work, and they had two polar-opposite responses. The first one under-promised but over-delivered, eventually following his father's wishes. The second one pretended to be obedient but failed. The indictment on the Pharisees is unmistakable: it's not what you promise to do, but what you ultimately do, that matters most.

The second shot comes in the parable of the tenant farmers (Matthew 21:33-46). The master entrusted the harvest to the farmers, in exchange for the privilege of living on the land. They had only one job: do the work, be faithful to the task, and give the owner what was rightfully due him. But the servants overshot their authority and decided not only to rebel but to commit murder. When the master sent his own son to set things straight, the farmers killed him. The point Jesus is making is very clear: instead of following the commandments of God, producing fruit worthy of the Kingdom, they committed acts of violence against his son.

Then, without taking a breath, Jesus launches into the final blow. It is in the parable of the wedding feast that we hear of the generosity and lavish love of God, who has prepared a sumptuous feast for all to enjoy. But the ones who should have been most excited and most grateful were the ones who were shockingly indifferent. Instead of coming to the feast with great joy, those who were invited go about their business, completely ignoring the invitation. Instead of begging and pleading the invitees to come to the dinner, the master did an amazing thing. He expanded the guest list to include the ones that everyone else would ignore, those pushed to the fringes, the ones marginalized in society. They came to the dinner with great eagerness and appreciation.

So, what is better, Jesus asks the people: To over-promise and under-deliver, like the Pharisees, or to come to come to a place of obedience in the end? To be given the privilege of living in the master's kingdom, only to rebel against him? Or to be faithful to the task to which we have been called, and to bear fruit in the fields, regardless of the cost?

To ignore the privilege of being part of God's family, and choose instead to live life on our own terms? Or to recognize the amazing gift that it is to be invited to such a feast, and dare to approach the banquet hall of God, no matter our weaknesses and shortcomings?

It certainly seems that as Jesus is addressing the Pharisees with this powerful string of indictments, he is addressing all of us.

Unfortunately for the Pharisees, these parables only emboldened their resolve to do away with Jesus. Maybe they didn't appreciate being called out so provocatively. It's possible no one had ever called them on their hypocrisy, let alone in public. Maybe they had never met their match until Jesus showed up, and it caught them flat-footed. Maybe they were not ready for a deep philosophical debate about the subject of authority. They thought they were following the rules, abiding by the laws, and adhering to the standards that had preserved their piety and their power for generations. The idea that Jesus could come along and claim allegiance to an authority even higher than their traditional perspective . . . well, that was too hard for them to understand.

It can be very hard to change for the better. Anyone who has ever been confronted with something detrimental in life that needs to be addressed knows that tackling one's inner shadows is difficult. Surrender usually gives way to self-defense and self-reliance, all in an effort toward self-preservation.

But as much as we might think of Jesus' delivery of these three successive parables as one of anger and retribution, maybe we can see it instead as being offered in love. It's the kind of love that intervenes when a loved one is doing a thorough job of self-destruction. The kind of love that speaks the truth, even though it hurts. The kind of love that is not willing to ignore the faults of someone you care about, but dares to enter the fray and engage the difficulty, right at the core.

It's the kind of love that a master has in sending his own son to the fields to talk to the farmers, knowing it will likely get tougher before it gets better.

It's the love that God has for you and me.

God, thank you for the privilege of being a part of your kingdom. Help me never to take that for granted, and to live up to the responsibilities to which you have called me. Help me to reach out in love to those who are pushed to the fringes of society. Amen.

Which of these three parables do you resonate with the most today?

DAY 36

Matthew 23:37-39; 25:31-46; Luke 13:34-35; 19:41-44

RETHINKING POWER

There are many things we learn about Jesus throughout the Gospels. There are many stories that describe his love and compassion, his tenacity for justice and equality, and his commitment to his mission. But there are only a few occasions when we experience the emotional side of Jesus, the part of him that reminds us just how human he was.

It's here, mere days from his arrest and death, that he stands on the outskirts of the city of Jerusalem and exhibits the all-too-human characteristic of lament.

"Jerusalem, Jerusalem," he calls out, just like a mother longing for her children to call in the middle of the night to remind her that they are okay. In fact, he uses the maternal image of a hen, longing to protect her brood, except he comes to this realization: he cannot force people to do what is necessary to protect themselves from harm.

The question of God's relationship to suffering and evil is one of the greatest hurdles for people of faith. There are many ways to ask the question, and many voices who have asked it. But it always winds up being a variation of the same three components: if God is 1) all-loving and 2) all-powerful, then 3) why are there suffering and evil in the world?

There is no easy way to make all three pieces fit together, so we have to make some adjustments. First, we might choose to adjust our expectations that God is all loving. But that's simply not an option here, is it? For if God is not all-loving, then we have a bigger problem than we thought.

Some people have tried to question the third piece in the equation, which is the reality of suffering and evil in the world. Some have tried to say that suffering and evil are not all that bad after all, especially if they help us build character, teach us to trust, or correct us from wrongdoing. Like a parent who tells us, "This is going to hurt me more than it hurts you," some people try to temper the severity of suffering by making it redemptive and corrective.

But try telling that to a parent who has had to bury a child or a family who has lost everything in a tornado. Sometimes, suffering is just suffering and there is no sugarcoating it.

So maybe the place to find wiggle room in this difficult dilemma is in the second element, which is the question of God being all-powerful.

What does it mean for God to be all-powerful? That God causes all things to happen? Maybe it's okay not believe that, especially if we believe in free will. After all, if humans have the power to choose and God doesn't treat us as puppets, then maybe God doesn't have all the power after all. Maybe God doesn't cause or even allow all things to happen. That seems to be Jesus' realization in today's Scripture passage. He longed for people to act in a certain way, but they were not willing.

Maybe God is powerful, not because God forces us to do certain things, but because God *calls* us to do certain things. Maybe God is powerful in the way God calls us to cooperation, with a persuasiveness that is greater than any other force in the world. Maybe God is powerful in the way God identifies with our suffering and ultimately transforms it—so that we can be agents of healing for the world.

Maybe God's power is best seen on a cross.

In other words, maybe God's power is not an ability to make things happen or keep things from happening, but in God's constant and faithful activity in luring, wooing, and persuading human beings to choose the better rather than the worse. Maybe God has more persuasive power than any other in the world.

Aesop tells a fable that illustrates this difference in power.

> The North Wind and the Sun had a quarrel about which of them was the stronger. While they were disputing with much heat and bluster, a Traveler passed along the road wrapped in a cloak.

"Let us agree," said the Sun, "that he is the stronger who can strip that Traveler of his cloak."

"Very well," growled the North Wind, and at once sent a cold, howling blast against the Traveler.

With the first gust of wind the ends of the cloak whipped about the Traveler's body. But he immediately wrapped it closely around him, and the harder the Wind blew, the tighter he held it to him. The North Wind tore angrily at the cloak, but all his efforts were in vain.

Then the Sun began to shine. At first his beams were gentle, and in the pleasant warmth after the bitter cold of the North Wind, the Traveler unfastened his cloak and let it hang loosely from his shoulders. The Sun's rays grew warmer and warmer. The man took off his cap and mopped his brow. At last he became so heated that he pulled off his cloak, and, to escape the blazing sunshine, threw himself down in the welcome shade of a tree by the roadside.[1]

It's not about having all the power. It's about having the right kind of power.

God, thank you for your power and love. Teach me to empathize with those in need, that I might be an agent of healing and strength for others. Amen.

How difficult is it to think of God's power in this way? What difference would it make for you to do so?

---

1 *The Aesop for Children, with Pictures by Milo Winter* (Chicago: Rand McNally and Company, 1919), 109.

DAY 37

Matthew 26:6-16; Mark 14:3-11

THE SILVER AND THE OINTMENT

Looming in the shadows is Judas Iscariot, the antagonist of the stories of Holy Week. Matthew 26:14-15 and Mark 14:10-11 record that infamous moment he went to the chief priests to betray Jesus for thirty pieces of silver. He becomes the betrayer who did Jesus in, the villain of the story.

But the Gospels are strangely silent on exactly *why* Judas did what he did. What was his motivation?

Earlier in my life, I was perfectly content to say, "Well, Satan took him over, told him to betray Jesus, and so he did." But since then, I've added a whole range of possibilities to the list. Perhaps Judas did it out of greed. Maybe he was tired of living day to day without financial security, tired of living off the hospitality of others, and he decided to build up his nest egg a bit. Perhaps he did it out of jealousy. Maybe he was tired of all the attention afforded to his master and the very little that was paid to him.

Maybe he did it out of disappointment. Maybe he was frustrated that the revolution had not begun and his dreams of political freedom from the Romans had not yet started. Maybe he thought that it was time for a new leader.

Or maybe Judas didn't intend to kill Jesus at all. Maybe he just wanted to "force his hand" a little. Perhaps Judas thought if he could push Jesus a little, Jesus would give in and become the kind of leader many were expecting him to be. The list of possibilities could go on and on.

Maybe the reason the Bible chooses not to elaborate on the motivation of Judas is that this would make things much too easy for us. If the Bible were to say that Judas betrayed Jesus out of greed, for example, then the message would be simple: don't be greedy, don't be jealous, or don't set yourself up for disappointment. Those kinds of straightforward motivations would make it easier for us to dismiss.

But the Scripture's silence in this matter would suggest that we can fill in the blank with our own costly temptations. Whatever Judas's downfall was, we share in equal capacity to betray Jesus ourselves, whatever our motivation might be. The Gospels leave it intentionally wide open as if to say to each of us, "Insert your own motivation here."

In contrast, look at the other key character in the story, before we even get to Judas. In Matthew 26:6-13 and Mark 14:3-9, we hear about a woman. These Gospel writers don't tell us her name or her relationship to Jesus, or to Simon, the owner of the house. Like Judas, we only know what she does. She takes an alabaster jar of very expensive ointment and cracks it open over Jesus' head, pouring the ointment all over his body.

Jesus saw this action as a preparation for his own imminent death. But how did the woman really know this? The others were angry that she wasted a lot of money on that action. But why didn't the woman care?

Left to interpret the actions alone, we're sort of stumped over this woman's motivation. But as both Matthew and Mark set up the stories of this woman and Judas in contrast to each other, what we can discern is this lesson:

The way to counter betrayal is through worship. The way to prevent sins against Jesus is a sacrificial commitment to following Jesus.

If sin can be defined as the heart turned inward upon itself, then worship can be defined as the heart turned outward and poured out before Christ.

If we recognize, right up front, that we have just as much capacity to betray Jesus as Judas did, then we can also see that the way to avoid it is by giving ourselves in full commitment to Christ, regardless of the cost, just like this woman did.

Judas is forever remembered for his actions. If he ever wanted a legacy, he surely got one. He has been since remembered for his wicked actions and mysterious, evil motivations.

If a better legacy is what you desire in life, then look no further than to this woman for your example. According to Jesus, she would also be remembered forever—not for her selfish deeds, but for her irrational, extravagant sacrifice of discipleship. So great and so bold was the expression of her commitment that Jesus said, "I tell you the truth that, wherever in the whole world the good news is announced, what she's done will also be told in memory of her" (Mark 14:9).

How's that for a legacy? What would it be like to be remembered for that?

God, forgive me for the ways in which I offer you less than my fullest commitment. Reveal to me my penchant for acting like Judas, and help me to offer my whole life to Jesus, regardless of the cost. Amen.

How are you most prone to acting like Judas? How might God be calling you to give your full commitment to Jesus?

DAY 38

Matthew 26:17-30; Mark 14:12-25;
Luke 22:7-20; John 13:1-17

MAUNDY THURSDAY: FOUR IMPORTANT VERBS

My grammar teacher in eighth grade was one of the most significant influences in my education, and she helped me at a young age learn to improve my writing. She taught me how to diagram sentences, fall in love with words, and appreciate good writing. One of the best pieces of advice she ever gave me was this:

Pay attention to your verbs.

Master your use of verbs, she said, and your writing will flourish. The most descriptive writing does not depend on nouns or adjectives. But if you find the right verb, in just the right place, for just the right reason—then the wow factor emerges. Your writing launches to new heights.

I can't say I'm a master of that technique yet, but I do believe she was right. Verbs are important.

Apparently, they were also important to the New Testament writers.

Four of the most important verbs in the Christian vocabulary are in the Scripture story for today. These four words occur in Matthew, Mark, and Luke as they describe what happened during the Last Supper. When Paul wrote about Communion and its meaning for the Church, he used similar language (1 Corinthians 11:23-24a): "The Lord Jesus, on the night he was betrayed, took bread, and when he had given thanks, he broke it" (NIV).

Took. Blessed. Broke. Gave.

Henri Nouwen was one of the most significant spiritual writers in the twentieth century. In his classic book *Life of the Beloved*, he expands our understanding of those four verbs by inviting us to see them not just in relation to what Jesus did to the bread, but what Jesus is doing in us.

For if Jesus was the bread of the world, and if we are called to be made in the image of that same Jesus day by day, then what would it look like for us—you and me, ordinary people—to be the very bread that Jesus takes, blesses, breaks, and gives?

First, we would remember that we have been *taken* by God. In a sense, we have indeed been taken. At the moment of our baptism, God made a claim on our lives. When the waters of baptism touched us, God said, "You are mine. The world will try to get its hands on you, but I won't let it; my grace will be at work in and through your life to lead on a path of full relationship with me." You are not your own; you belong to God.

What's more, you've been *blessed*. You are not just God's child, but you have been given a unique composition that makes you unlike any other. Your skills, passions, connections with people, background, experience, and perspectives make you specially equipped to fulfill a particular purpose in the world. And all of this has come entirely from God's grace and favor, not through your own efforts, but as a gift from God.

And you have been *broken*. Sometimes, there is no way for you to experience the fullness of God's blessings without going through some process of struggle and trial. You have been broken, and you can identify those moments in your life in which you were at your lowest, only to discover that those became pivot points, critical transitional periods that enabled you to experience utter dependence and trust in God.

And finally, like that bread, God has *given* us. We have been given to the world to meet the needs of people who hunger for something joyful, loving, and peaceful. You are not here simply to meet your own needs but to be given out, distributed, to those who would seek to find Jesus for themselves.

So, with all due gratitude to my eighth-grade grammar teacher, remember the power of these words: *take*, *bless*, *break*, and *give*. As we make this final turn toward the finish line of Holy Week, remember what Jesus did for you and what God is calling you to do in response to Jesus.

God, I am but bread in your hands. You have taken me, blessed me, and broken me. I offer myself to your purposes, that I may be given out to the world. Amen.

Think about each of these four important words. When have there been times in your life when you could identify with each one?

DAY 39

Matthew 26:1–27:56; Mark 14:1–15:41;
Luke 22:1–23:49; John 18:1–19:37

GOOD FRIDAY: A TALE OF TWO BOWLS

In William Shakespeare's play *Macbeth,* Lady Macbeth uttered those famous words, "Out, damned spot! Out, I say!" She was so overcome with guilt from her part in the murder of King Duncan that she began hallucinating about having blood on her hands. Despite her constant hand washing, she could not remove the stain from her conscience. Little could William Shakespeare have known when he wrote the play that over four hundred years later, in 2006, researchers at Northwestern University would coin the term "Macbeth Effect" to describe the psychosomatic link between a person's guilty conscience and personal hygiene.

Researchers asked a group of students to remember a time in their lives when they had committed some unethical deed, such as betraying a friend. They asked a second group to remember a time they performed a noble deed, like returning lost money. Afterwards, researchers offered members of the two groups the choice of a gift: either a pencil or an antiseptic wipe. Amazingly, people asked to relive an unethical episode in their lives were twice as likely to accept the antiseptic wipe and use it to wash their hands.

What is it about washing hands that somehow clears a conscience of wrongdoing?

Consider Pontius Pilate, who followed his sentencing of Jesus to death by washing his hands. Perhaps he had grown weary of the debate and the competing voices between his own conscience and the Jerusalem crowds. Perhaps he had sensed Jesus' innocence but cowered in fear of the growing mob. Perhaps we would want to give Pilate some credit for at least considering the correct choice during his deliberation. But when he washed his hands, he absolved himself of any opportunity to do what was costly, what was risky, and what was right.

Anglican priest Morton Kelsey, in his essay "*The Cross and the Cellar*," wrote:

> Pilate receives most of the blame for Jesus' death, and yet Pilate didn't want to crucify the man. Why did Pilate condemn Jesus? Because Pilate was a coward. He cared more about his comfortable position than he did about justice. He didn't have the courage to stand for what he knew was right. It was because of this relatively small flaw in Pilate's character that Jesus died on a cross. Whenever you and I are willing to sacrifice someone else for our own benefit, whenever we don't have the courage to stand up for what we see is right, we step into the same course that Pilate took.[1]

That is a biting accusation against Pilate. If it makes us squirm, it is because we can see our own propensity to be as guilty as Pilate. We would be remiss if we relegated Pilate to a distance, thinking that because he was a person of power, prestige, and authority, we are so different that we could never do anything as vile as he did. The truth is, we are not much different.

His decision was antithetical to the meaning of the cross, which calls us to take the narrow, more complicated path. Whereas the Pilates of this world will choose what is easy and expedient, followers of Jesus are called to live a *cruciform* life, a life of service and self-surrender. In other words, a life shaped by a willingness to take up one's cross. In contrast to the way of violence and appeasement, disciples are called to peace, self-sacrifice, and love.

Ultimately, the hand-washing bowl of Pilate is a direct contrast to the foot-washing bowl of Jesus. On the night before he died, just hours before Pilate washed his hands, Jesus assumed the role of a servant and washed the disciples' feet. And then, he gave them a new commandment: "Love each other. Just as I have loved you, so you also must love each other. This is how everyone will know that you are my disciples, when you love each other" (John 13:34-35).

On this Good Friday, ponder this question: Are you a foot washer or a hand washer? Will you offer yourself in self-giving love to others, or will you choose the less complicated way of self-centeredness? Will you follow a road that is marked by cowardice or a road that leads to a cross? Will you choose a love for power or the path of powerless love?

As we make the turn toward Holy Saturday and finish our Lenten journey with the glory of Easter, remember the words of the great hymn "Rock of Ages, Cleft for Me":

> Nothing in my hand I bring,
> simply to the cross I cling;
> naked, come to thee for dress;
> helpless, look to thee for grace;
> foul, I to the fountain fly;
> wash me, Savior, or I die.[2]

God, thank you for the example of Pilate, which reveals to me my own sinful capacity. Help me to live more into the example of Jesus, who gave himself for others in servanthood and humility.

When was there a time in your life when your guilt over a past action felt like a stain you could not scrub away?

---

1 Morton T. Kelsey, "The Cross and the Cellar," in *The Cross: Meditations on the Seven Last Words of Christ* (New York: Paulist, 1980). Quoted in *Bread and Wine: Readings for Lent and Easter* (Orbis, 2005), 210-211.

2 "Rock of Ages, Cleft for Me," Augustus M. Toplady; *The United Methodist Hymnal* (Nashville: The United Methodist Publishing House, 1989), 361, stanza 3.

DAY 40

Matthew 27:57-61; Mark 15:42-47;
Luke 23:50-56; John 19:38-42

HOLY SATURDAY: GOD ALREADY AT WORK

For those closest to Jesus, I suspect they got very little sleep during the night after the Crucifixion. They had to be experiencing a perfect storm of intense emotional fallout as a result of what happened to Jesus. There was the grief, of course. Their dear, beloved teacher and friend, the one who had utterly changed their lives after three and a half years of adventurous ministry, had been brutally ripped away from them. There was also the confusion. How could someone so pure and holy, so loving and generous, so innocent and sincere, be executed by the highest levels of power, in the most humiliating public way? This was no way for anyone so perfect to be treated.

There also had to be fear. Now that their leader was gone, his followers knew that surely the authorities would be coming after them next. That's usually the way it went with uprisings, and that is surely how the Roman officials characterized this movement by Jesus. Now that he was out of the way, the military officials would certainly be hunting them down, lest any of them try to ascend to leadership and reignite the cause.

All the followers of Jesus must have had a very sleepless night.

Holy Saturday is a peculiar day in the drama of Holy Week. Just about every day is filled with drama and vivid remembrance. Palm Sunday has the pageantry and the procession. Maundy Thursday has the Last Supper, the foot-washing, and the commandment to love. Good Friday has the passion narrative, the extinguishing of lights, the retelling of the Crucifixion.

But Holy Saturday is a pause. It is a chance to take a breath. It is a chance to do little else but reflect on what has happened in us and through us throughout this entire Lenten journey, in light of what happened just one day prior.

Consider what has been happening to you throughout these past six weeks of embracing the uncertain. What difficult things have you learned about yourself that you were reluctant to acknowledge before?

Where have you experienced the limits of your own strength and wisdom?

When have you had to name and confront your deepest fears?

Where have you longed for joy amid pain, and peace amid conflict?

When have you acknowledged your imperfections and failures?

Where has there been grief or loss?

These are all elements of the experience of Holy Saturday. It just might be the most important day of Holy Week to prepare you for Easter.

Because here's the deal. By the time we get to that glorious Easter morning, most of the Gospel writers will attest: the resurrection of Jesus has already begun, even before people realized it. When the women arrive at the tomb in Mark, Luke, and John, they discover that the stone that sealed the tomb *had already* been rolled away. In other words, resurrection had already started even before they showed up.

What that means is that God is working in your life *right now*, already working without your realization, to raise you up in Christ to new life, new hope, and new possibility. God does not wait for our awareness before doing the work of resurrection. God does not need our acknowledgment, or even our understanding, before doing a new thing. That includes whatever God is doing in you.

In Wesleyan terms, this concept is called the prevenient grace of God. It is the work of God that begins from the moment we take our first breath, which lures us and woos us into a saving acceptance of God before we are aware of it. It is the activity of a God who, in the words of one of my spiritual mentors, "loves us enough to meet us where we are, and loves us too much to leave us there."

Good Friday was yesterday. Easter morning is to come. For now, this Saturday is holy. For God is already at work.

God, thank you for Holy Saturday. I pray that this is a time of rest and renewal, as I await with great anticipation my awareness of your resurrecting work in my life. Amen.

What are the top lessons you have discovered throughout these last forty days of this Lenten journey? What are you hoping to experience on Easter Sunday?

EASTER

Matthew 28:1-20

ACT FREE!

Matthew 28:2 says that suddenly "there was a great earthquake."

The funny thing about earthquakes, of course, is you can't plan for them. With hurricanes, you follow prediction cones. With tornadoes, you hear the sirens. With floods, you watch the waters rise. But earthquakes happen without warning, without lead time, out of the blue.

That's the way it is with life. Just when you think your life is humming along, just Goldilocks-like, not great, but not too bad, the earthquake hits.

The boss calls you into his office. The doctor calls and says the news is not good. The police knock on your door in the middle of the night.

We don't know for sure what the women were thinking and feeling when they showed up at the tomb on Easter morning, but there was no way they could have been prepared for the earthquake when they got there. That's what life is like: a surprise around every corner, a curveball out of the blue.

When an earthquake happens, it's usually bad news.

That's what made this Easter earthquake so surprising. It's the key to rediscovering the newsworthiness of this good news for us. Just this once, for the only time in history, an earthquake happened to bring good news, not bad. It brought an announcement of new life, not death. Of hope, not despair.

The messengers said, "He isn't here, because he's been raised from the dead, just as he said" (Matthew 28:6). Now, if this news is as great as the Gospels would lead us to believe, then it should be enough to shock us into a whole new appreciation of God's love, push us into a new way of living, and move us to become an alternative community to the suffering and evil in the world.

In other words, this Easter earthquake is the sound of victory in a world full of defeat, and that ought to make a difference.

But maybe, just like the women, we aren't ready to understand it, let alone receive it.

Remember, their first response was not cheer. It was fear. They were so frightened that the angel had to calm them down and tell them not to be afraid.

Look at the Roman officials. Their first response was not belief but denial. They were so determined to rationalize away the Resurrection that they covered it up with a conspiracy theory.

Look at countless others at the end of the Gospel. Matthew says there were some who doubted the good news.

That's the amazing thing about the good news of Easter. We are so used to the bad news that even when there's news of victory and new life, we respond in fear, or disbelief, or doubt.

Even as we gather with others on this Easter morning, we just come to look. So often we miss just how good the good news really is.

Theologian Alister MacGrath recounts a story he once heard from a man who served in the army during World War II. He was a prisoner of war in a Japanese prison camp. Day after day, the man wondered whether he was going to die or live to see another day. He wondered about his fallen comrades, whether they were still alive, whether they were even there in the same prison camp. He wondered how the war was going on out in the rest of the world. Were they winning? Were they losing? What was happening?

Then one day, the man received word. One of the other prisoners was listening to a short-wave radio one day when the word was broadcast. The Japanese had just surrendered. The Allied forces had won. Victory has just been guaranteed. He sat there, having heard the news, in disbelief. Then he rejoiced.

Then the man realized that nothing about his situation had really changed. It would take days and weeks for the prisoners to be found in their prison camp in Singapore and eventually be released. In the meantime, they were still there living with rationed food, in inhumane conditions, in the presence of their tormentors and their captors.

But even though their day-to-day problems had not changed, there was something about the guarantee of victory that changed their perspective and their outlook. They knew that even though their situation seemed the same, in the grand scheme of things, victory was assured, and they were not going to be in this condition forever.

Soon, the attitude of the prisoners changed. They were still prisoners, but they acted free. They celebrated, they sang songs. They laughed and they cried together. For they knew that their deliverance was assured.[1]

That is what the resurrection of Jesus does. It shocks us like an earthquake, because that's what it takes to get our attention, to change the way we look at the world and live our lives. Because of the victory we have in Christ, we can choose to live victoriously. This is the good news of Easter. And you may not have realized just how much you really needed to hear it.

But the real question now is what difference it will make in your life. Now that you *are* free in Christ, will you *act* free in Christ?

The good news of Easter is that Christ is risen. The task of Easter is to live in that victory over sin and death that has been given to us in Christ. It means acting like we are free and living like we are free. It means remembering that Jesus is always with us.

God, I am amazed and grateful for your resurrecting power at work in my life. Thank you for raising me up with Jesus, in whom I find new hope and possibility. Help me to act as one who is free from the power of sin and death. Amen.

In what way has this journey of Lent and Easter offered you surprising good news? What difference will the good news of Easter make in your life today and in days to come?

---

1 Alister E. McGrath, *What Was God Doing on the Cross?* (Grand Rapids: Zondervan, 1992), 54.